Stories We
Tell Ourselves

Also by Richard Holloway

Stories We Tell Ourselves

Making Meaning in a Meaningless Universe

RICHARD HOLLOWAY

CANONGATE

First published in Great Britain, the USA and Canada in 2020 by
Canongate Books Ltd, 14 High Street, Edinburgh EH1 1TE

Published in the USA by Publishers Group West and
in Canada by Publishers Group Canada

canongate.co.uk

1

British Library Cataloguing-in-Publication Data
A catalogue record for this book is available
on request from the British Library

ISBN 978 1 78689 993 4

Typeset in Garamond MT by
Palimpsest Book Production Ltd, Falkirk, Stirlingshire

Printed and bound in Great Britain by Clays Ltd, Elcograf S.p.A.

For Jim and Helen Mein

CONTENTS

PROLOGUE

Whether or not we acknowledge it, we all live by the stories we tell ourselves to explain the mystery of our existence, the suffering that accompanies it, and the certain death that concludes it. But our stories do more than offer us explanations for the mystery of existence. They also supply us with rules for living the lives we have been thrust into. The difficulty is in identifying the story we are actually living by. That has certainly been my problem, and I am writing this book to try to resolve it. What story am I trying to live by, and what are its consequences? In a collection of essays published in 1979 called *The White Album*, Joan Didion captured the main issue:

> We tell ourselves stories in order to live . . . We live entirely . . . by the imposition of a narrative line upon disparate images, by the 'ideas' with which we have learned to freeze the shifting phantasmagoria which is our actual experience. Or at least we do for a while. I am talking here about a time when I began to doubt the premises of all the stories I had ever told myself, a common condition but one I found troubling.

Here Didion expresses the human dilemma: our need for stories to live by, while acknowledging how precarious and uncertain they are. She then describes the incident that prompted this beginning of doubt in the stories she had told herself.

> I . . . read, in the papers . . . the story of Betty Lansdown Fouquet, a 26-year-old woman with faded blond hair who put her five-year-old daughter out to die on the center divider of Interstate 5 some miles south of the last Bakersfield exit. The child, whose fingers had to be pried loose from the Cyclone fence when she was rescued twelve hours later by the California Highway Patrol, reported that she had run after the car carrying her mother and stepfather and brother and sister for 'a long time.' Certain of these images did not fit into any narrative I knew.[1]

I know that feeling of uncertainty and discomfort. The Christian religion has been one of the most prolific tellers of the stories by which many of us have tried to live. But what story can it possibly tell that will account for the ancient and abiding sorrows of children? That is the great stumbling block many of us can't climb over in our search for the meaning or purpose of the universe. I have to confess that my discomfort is no longer that of the confident believer who has to fit that incident into the story of how a good God could have come up with a universe in which that kind of thing happens every day. Even when I was telling myself that story, I was never persuaded by the explanations offered by theologians. They demonstrated what to me has always been a weakness in most theological systems: a discomfort with uncertainty that impels a compulsion to explain or account for every mystery under the sun.

I wonder now if this is not a consequence of the male dominance of religious and political systems down the ages. The feminist writer Rebecca Solnit coined the term 'mansplaining' to describe the experience of listening to a man condescendingly explaining something to her he thinks she cannot possibly understand. It's a well-known phenomenon. Solnit attributes it to a combination of overconfidence and cluelessness, a not infrequent combination in the male of the human species. It is rife in Christianity, which has a passion for proclaiming its confident solutions to all the existential puzzles that beset us. I wonder also if male impatience hasn't a lot to do with this rush to judgement and decision. Is it a frustration with the silence of God? An embarrassment? Like those silences that sometimes fall between two people on a long journey which one of them is compelled to fill with nervous chatter? There is certainly a lot of chatter in Christianity. It suggests an unease somewhere, a fear of the void that lies beneath us.

I have always thought believing Jews were more honest about the problem of suffering than believing Christians. There is a scene in Elie Wiesel's holocaust novel *Night* that casts a dark light on the problem. He tells us that one day in Auschwitz they saw three prisoners in chains, one of them a child. He writes:

The SS seemed more preoccupied, more worried, than usual. To hang a child in front of thousands of onlookers was not a small matter. The head of the camp read the verdict. All eyes were on the child. He was pale, almost calm, but he was biting his lip as he stood in the shadow of the gallows . . .

The three condemned prisoners together stepped onto the chairs. In unison, the nooses were placed around their necks . . .

At the signal, the three chairs were tipped over . . .

Then came the march past the victims. The two men were no longer alive. Their tongues were hanging out, swollen and bluish. But the third rope was still moving: the child, too light, was still breathing . . .

And so he remained for more than half an hour, lingering between life and death, writhing before our eyes. And we were forced to look at him at close range. He was still alive when I passed him. His tongue was still red, his eyes not yet extinguished.

Behind me, I heard . . . 'For God's sake, where is God?'

And from within me, I heard a voice answer:

'Where He is? This is where – hanging here from this gallows . . .'[2]

This could mean that in Auschwitz God died, and we are alone in a pitiless universe. Or that in the sorrows of children, God – supposing there is a God – is on the gallows with them, twisting on the rope. It has to be one or the other. God is either dead or in some sense helpless. I just can't make up my mind which. And that's why I'm with the rabbis in Auschwitz who put God on trial, found him guilty and then said the evening prayer. Here's a prayer they might have used, translated from the Yiddish of Kadya Molodowsky:

O God of mercy
For the time being
Choose another people.
We are tired of death, tired of corpses,
We have no more prayers.
For the time being
Choose another people.
We have run out of blood
For victims,
Our houses have been turned into desert,
The earth lacks space for tombstones,
There are no more lamentations
Nor songs of woe
In the ancient texts.
. . . God of Mercy
Grant us one more blessing –
Take back the divine glory of our genius.[3]

I am moved by those who believe in God like that, but reject the divine justification story. Its best expression in literature was given by Ivan Karamazov in Dostoevsky's great novel. Ivan has collected an unbearable anthology of the sufferings of Russian children. He tells his devout brother Alyosha that he positively maintains 'that this quality exists in much of mankind – this love of torturing children . . . It is precisely the defencelessness of these children that tempts the torturers'. He goes on:

I want to be there when everyone suddenly finds out what it was all for. All religions in the world are based on this desire, and I am a believer. But then there are the children, and what am I going to do with them? That is the question I cannot resolve . . . there are hosts of questions, but I've taken only the children, because here what I say is irrefutably clear . . . if everyone must suffer, in order to buy eternal harmony with their suffering, pray tell me what children have to do with it? It's quite incomprehensible why they should have to suffer, and why they should buy harmony with their suffering . . . It's not that I don't accept God, Alyosha. I just most respectfully return him the ticket.[4]

It is worth spending a minute to think about the collision of stories implied in Ivan's outburst, because it is something that comes up again and again in human experience. The stories we tell ourselves to make sense of our lives often come into conflict with each other, so we either choose to live with the contradiction or we abandon one of the stories. This classic dilemma was noticed by the sixth-century Christian philosopher Boethius, who described it as a . . .

. . . discord in the pact of things,
This endless war twixt truth and truth,
That singly hold, yet give the lie
To him who seeks to yoke them both . . .[5]

Ivan's problem was that he was unable to live with the discord and was forced to give up one of the stories he'd been told. The founding story behind his outrage is the existence of a good, all-powerful God, whose creatures we are. But within that story another story has to follow immediately in order to account for the existence of suffering in the world created by such a God. In the passage from *The Brothers Karamazov* I have already quoted, Ivan describes the justificatory story as an 'eternal harmony' that could only be purchased at the price of such human sorrow.

> I don't want harmony, for the love of mankind I don't want it. I want to remain with unrequited suffering. I'd rather remain with my unrequited suffering and my unquenched indignation, *even if I am wrong*. Besides, they have put too high a price on harmony; we can't afford to pay so much for admission. And therefore I hasten to return my ticket.[6]

This is the element in the story Ivan rejects not in disbelief but in revulsion. He wants no dealings with a God who can come up with a scheme that involves the suffering of children, even if their pain is to be justified when the meaning of the universe is finally revealed.

> . . . pray tell me what children have to do with it? It's quite incomprehensible why they . . . should buy harmony with their suffering.

So he respectfully returns him the ticket. This response is sometimes described as angry atheism, as opposed to the cooler, rational type of atheism that sees no point in getting upset at Someone who doesn't exist. But Ivan tells us he is not an atheist. He is a God-hater, a very different thing. Another Russian said something similar, this time a real not a fictional one. The novelist Kingsley Amis once asked the poet Yevgeny Yevtushenko if he believed in God. No, he replied, before adding: actually, it's more that I hate the bastard. Ivan was more polite than Yevtushenko, but he felt the same way and registered his membership in an ancient and honourable company of believers who

. . . are tired of death, tired of corpses
. . . have no more prayers . . .

and just want God to leave them alone.

My dilemma is the opposite of Ivan's. Ivan accepted God but wanted to keep his distance from him and the community of faith that bowed to him. I am not sure I do accept God, or how God has been traditionally defined or understood. That's one prong of my dilemma. But the other is that, unlike Ivan Karamazov, I find myself unable to tear up the ticket of my membership in one of the communities that worships the God I don't think I believe in – the Christian Church.

I tried to do that twenty years ago. I thought I'd thrown away the ticket for ever. But slowly over the following twenty years I found myself slipping back into the place where my prayers had once been valid. Gradually, I found myself at home again, my ticket frayed at the edges, smudged and bleared, but reclaimed. So, what kind of confused story am I trying to tell myself these days? I am hoping that by writing this book I'll find out.

And I want to return to Joan Didion to help me. As a writer, Didion became an explorer of what she calls 'the shifting phantasmagoria' of actual human experience.

'Phantasmagoria' is a disconcerting word to use, and a writer as careful as Didion won't have used it casually. It comes loosely from the Greek for ghastly presences encountered in public spaces. It was coined to describe a kind of horror show that was designed to terrify people. It used what was called a 'magic lantern' hidden at the back of a darkened room that projected terrifying images onto a screen in front of a suggestible and often-hysterical audience. Didion is saying that the horror show is art imitating life, the way good art always does. It represents what she calls 'our actual experience'. In this case, the fact that we live in a world in which a young mother can put her five-year-old daughter out to die on a Californian highway.

I don't think our difficulty is in finding a story that will make sense of an event like that. After all, the story we choose may be that no sense *can* be made of it, because the universe itself makes no sense, has no meaning, is just a weird, indifferent process in which terrible things happen every day. No, I don't think our problem is with the *differences* in the stories we tell. It's that telling *stories* is not always what we think we are doing when we are doing it. That's because the word 'story' is inevitably associated with 'fiction', stuff we make up. But fictions can be true or false. True in the sense that they tell us something valid about the human condition, false in the sense that we can wilfully misread them. Religion is full of true fictions, stories that carry meanings we have to work for, much the way spies have to interpret the coded messages they receive from headquarters. The trouble is that too many people fail to understand that reading is an interpretive art, that stories can carry many different layers of meaning, and that the most obvious or *literal* reading may be the furthest from the intended truth. Nowhere is this truer than in learning to read religious stories, something I'll spend a bit of time doing in this book.

But it is not just religious stories that require interpretation and understanding. All our stories do, particularly the ones we think aren't stories, aren't *fictions*. *We* think we are engaging with *reality*. *We* are offering objective descriptions of the way things are. *We* are pinning down the facts. But there is always a catch, a caveat. The catch is that while this is the truth of what *we* are doing, it is not what others are up to. Their efforts often *are* 'just stories', stuff they made up, comforting illusions they wanted to believe in, while our stories are 'the truth'. How well I know that game. I've played it against others, and others have played it against me. It's a favourite game in religion and politics, the oldest lantern shows in history.

But who can blame us for playing these games without being aware that that's what we are doing? To use Martin Heidegger's word for our situation, we were all 'thrown' or shot into a universe that does not explain itself, so we are left trying to figure it out for ourselves as we go along. Here I must pause for a moment to remember that this great philosopher, who helped many of us make sense of our existence, also embraced one of the vilest stories humanity has ever told itself, when he sided with the Nazi regime in Germany in the 1930s. A particularly ugly detail in the Heidegger phantasmagoria is that some of his most devoted students were Jews, including his young lover Hannah Arendt, yet he never uttered a word of blame about the Holocaust that destroyed six million Jewish people in the Nazi death camps. As the poet W.H. Auden said of W.B. Yeats, that's because Heidegger was 'silly like us'. The great thinkers and system-builders often are. That is why I prefer poets and other artists who are content to *express* the human condition, to philosophers and theologians who grab me by the arm and insist on explaining it to me. Here's Auden writing on 1 September 1939, as we plunged ourselves into yet another horror show:

> Faces along the bar
> Cling to their average day:
> The lights must never go out,
> The music must always play,
> All the conventions conspire
> To make this fort assume
> The furniture of home;
> Lest we should see where we are,
> Lost in a haunted wood,
> Children afraid of the night
> Who have never been happy or good.[7]

A haunted wood is a good metaphor for the universe into which, without any choice in the matter, I was propelled at birth and from which I shall be expelled at death, echoing Beckett's words from Godot that we are all born astride the grave. As I get near the edge of the trees, something in me wants to reconcile the contradictory stories I told myself as I made my way. But that's not all I want to do. As well as reconciling and finding space for contradictions, there are some stories I want to resist. These are the stories that channel humanity's innate instinct for violence, that strange lust in us to destroy the stranger, the different, the other.

I am conscious of the presence of such violence in my own lived experience. Though I was occasionally involved in physical violence as a boy and young man, most of my aggression as an adult has been expended in disagreement over ideas, usually religious and political ideas. I am aware of the fury that can accompany disagreements of this kind. I have felt it myself and been disturbed by it. Nietzsche and Freud have helped me understand it. Nietzsche thought that the psychic pain that often overwhelms us as we make our way through the haunted wood impels us to identify an enemy or hate-figure on whom we can vent our revenge for the sufferings we are undergoing.

> Every sufferer instinctively seeks a cause for his suffering; more exactly, an agent; still more specifically, a guilty agent who is susceptible to suffering – in short, some living thing upon which he can, on some pretext or other, vent his feelings, actually or in effigy: for the venting of his feelings represents the greatest attempt on the part of the suffering to win relief, anaesthesia, the narcotic he cannot help desiring to deaden pain of any kind.[8]

Freud went further than Nietzsche and noticed that our most likely scapegoats are neighbours or associates who betray marginal differences from us, onto whom we can fix reasons for our suffering. This is why some of the grimmest conflicts in history have been between communities that lived peacefully alongside each other for years, till some aggrieved person exploded a real or metaphorical bomb that blew apart centuries of tolerance. He called this phenomenon the 'narcissism of minor differences', and he said its root lay in the aggressiveness which civilisation had insisted we must sacrifice for the sake of the advantages it offered, but which was always there inside us, crouching below the surface, waiting for the occasion of its violent release. This is what he wrote:

> It is clearly not easy for men to give up the satisfaction of this inclination to aggression. They do not feel comfortable without it. The advantage which a comparatively small cultural group offers of allowing this instinct an outlet in the form of hostility against intruders is not to be despised. It is always possible to bind together a considerable number of people in love, so long as there are other people left over to receive the manifestations of their aggressiveness . . . I gave this phenomenon the name of 'the narcissism of minor differences' . . . We can see now that it is a convenient and relatively harmless satisfaction of the inclination to aggression, by means of which cohesion between the members of community is made easier.[9]

'Harmless satisfaction of the inclination to aggression' – unless you belong to the group that is its object at any particular moment in history, such as European Jews, the community Freud had in mind when he was writing this essay in 1930. Given the right circumstances, the 'harmless satisfaction of the inclination to aggression' against a marginal community can lead to the Holocaust of six million Jews in Nazi gas ovens in the twentieth century; or to the persecution of Irish Catholic immigrants in Scotland in the nineteenth and early twentieth centuries. An example from our own time in Britain is the state-sponsored persecution of the Windrush generation of West Indian immigrants, the effects of which are still reverberating as I write these words in 2019.

When you turn to the divisions in faith communities, you find that the narcissism of minor differences can be so microsurgical that it is impossible for outsiders to follow it. Let me offer an example not in a spirit of contempt, but of amused exasperation at minute differences in theological interpretation that once caused Christians to fight each other and still keeps them divided today. The issue concerns what happens to the bread and wine during a celebration of the central sacrament of the Christian Church, the Eucharist.

Do they *become* the body and blood of Jesus, or do they just *remind* Christians of his constant presence in their midst, as the main opposing theories have it? Including the two already noticed – labelled 'transubstantiationism' and 'memorialism' – six theories are offered to define the nature of the presence. The other four are 'consubstanti-ationism', 'transignificationism', 'transfinalisationism' and 'virtualism'. I'll leave it to interested readers to check out the definition of these awkward words for themselves; the point to register is that within the Church to this day there are Christians who won't share the sacrament with each other because they do not hold the right theory of its meaning. This is the narcissism of minor differences with a vengeance.

That said, something in me wants to understand and forgive Roman Catholics for refusing me the Eucharist and for believing that it is only valid in their celebrations. It shows how important the stories we tell ourselves are to our comfort and security in life. And why an important part of their power derives from the sense of superiority over others with which they endow us. Explore the stories we tell against each other, and you will discover that this is the magic ingredient. My religion is superior to yours. Or my rejection of religion is superior to your pathetic clinging to it. These are the games we play against each other; and no wonder. The Scottish philosopher David Hume captured our predicament when he told us we were placed in the world 'as in a great theatre, where the true springs and causes of every event are entirely concealed from us'. That is why it is no surprise that our imagination goes to work 'forming ideas of those powers on which we have so entire a dependence'.[10]

That was Hume's version of Auden's haunted wood, this mysterious existence into which we have all been thrust. No wonder we are often frightened and angry. No wonder we tell stories against each other. No wonder we elevate the minor differences between us into narratives of conflict and excommunication as we huddle together in the dark. But I am not writing this book to mock the differences in the stories we have told each other down the centuries. I am searching for a different way of listening to them, fumbling towards a new ecumenism of the meanings by which we interpret our common existence. But it will also be a personal exploration. My own intellectual history has been characterised by profound shifts and contradictions, yet I remain the same person. If I can find a way of reconciling myself to myself, maybe it will help others to do the same. The attempt will take me on a journey round the stories we have told ourselves to explain ourselves to ourselves, with all their fascinating contradictions and differences of interpretation. And I'll begin with the stories scientists now tell us about where *it* all came from.

PART I

IT OR THE UNIVERSE
OR EVERYTHING THAT IS

I

STORIES ABOUT
THE UNIVERSE

To return to Auden's phrase, what is the nature of the haunted wood we are lost in? And where did it come from? Or, to continue his metaphor, who planted it? These are the questions scientists try to answer; but even *their* stories keep changing. This was something a young physicist at Harvard started thinking about in the 1960s. While trying to account for the differences between the geocentric astronomy of Aristotle around 300 BCE and the heliocentric account offered by Isaac Newton 2,000 years later, it occurred to Thomas Kuhn that Aristotle's theories were not 'bad Newton', but different ways of looking at the same thing. He realised that we can't help seeing the world through the spectacles we wear: the circumstances that have conditioned us and the attitudes that have formed us; and we are largely unconscious of their presence or their effect. We don't realise that where we stand when we look at something affects not only *how* but *what* we see.

In his book *The Structure of Scientific Revolutions*, published in 1970, Kuhn suggested that what we think of as 'true' at any one time is always related to where we stand in history. He noticed how the history of science was characterised by periods of peaceful and normal research punctuated by epochs of crisis and transformation. When the going view had been stretched to its limits, it caused what Kuhn called a scientific revolution. Once the revolution had been established, what he called a new 'paradigm' rapidly evolved. And for the generation of scientists that followed, it became the inevitable way of seeing things and doing research – till the next revolution displaced it. 'Paradigms' were scientific theories or ways of looking at the world that fulfilled two requirements: they had to be 'sufficiently unprecedented to attract an enduring group of adherents away from competing modes of scientific activity', and they had to be 'sufficiently open-ended to leave all sorts of problems for the redefined group of practitioners to resolve'.[1] The history of science was the record of these contests and resolutions. He also mischievously observed that one of the factors in the advance of science into the new paradigm was the death of the scientists who had clung to the old one.

So: what is today's paradigm or science's current way of seeing the world? Since I am more at home with poetry than science, let me give the first word to a man who was both poet and scientist, Primo Levi:

> Fellow humans, to whom a year is a long time,
> A century a venerable goal,
> Struggling for your bread,
> Tired, fretful, tricked, sick, lost;
> Listen, and may it be mockery and consolation.
> Twenty billion years before now,
> Brilliant, soaring in space and time,

There was a ball of flame, solitary, eternal,
Our common father and our executioner.
It exploded, and every change began.
Even now the thin echo of this one reverse
    catastrophe
Resounds from the farthest reaches.
From that one spasm everything was born:
The same abyss that enfolds and challenges us,
The same time that spawns and defeats us,
Everything anyone has ever thought,
The eyes of every woman we have loved,
Suns by the thousands
And this hand that writes.[2]

I am told that Primo Levi exaggerated the age of the universe in his poem, but his exaggeration is understandable. The numbers are so huge as to be almost meaningless to creatures for whom living to a hundred 'is a venerable goal'. The current scientific paradigm tells us that the originating event happened over thirteen billion years ago. Here I have to be careful. I have promised myself that I will only put into words what I think I know or at least partly understand, so I am at a grave disadvantage here. Because I do not understand some of the things that scientists tell me about this originating event.

Though it stuns me, I think I can understand the vastness of the universe, which may contain as many as 140 *billion* galaxies. Bill Bryson helped me get my head round that unimaginable number when he suggested that if galaxies were frozen peas there would be enough of them to fill the Royal Albert Hall.[3] And that's only in the *visible* universe! I am told that there may be an infinite number of universes beyond our knowing, and that we have been lucky to arrive in the one whose particular chemistry enables us to exist.

The elements of which our bodies were formed, which made our evolution possible, were a consequence of all that grinding violence. They did not exist until the universe had reached a particular point in its expansion when the clouds of hydrogen and helium it released were cool enough to condense into the galaxies that formed the first stars. Stars are the great nuclear furnaces in which all these complex elements are made. Their metals and minerals and gases are released into space in colossal explosions that happen when the balance between the internal pressure of the star and its own force of gravity breaks down and the star explodes. All these processes – the forming of stars, the slow cooking of the elements, and their explosive release into space – took over ten billion years to complete.

Our earth is a fragment of stardust about five billion years old formed from the reverberations of one of these explosions. It orbits in the suburbs of one small galaxy in a universe of billions of galaxies. And it has remained hospitable to life for at least three-and-a-half billion years. This is a consequence of the stability of the sun, which has been burning long enough to allow life to evolve and flourish on our little planet.

The sun appears to us to be the largest and brightest of the stars, but it is actually one of the smallest and faintest. The illusion arises because of its comparative nearness to us – it is only ninety-three million miles away, while the next nearest star is nearly 300,000 times as far away, more than four light years. But without the heat from that violent, burning star we would not be here. And violent it certainly is. Scientists catch occasional glimpses of shock-waves and great tornadoes whipping round it at more than 100,000 miles per hour. As well as the sun's heat giving us life, it may be its heat that finally finishes us off. One theory offered to explain how our planet will die is that billions of years from now chemical activity within the sun will expand it to 250 times its present size, and fry us to a crisp in the process – though it now looks as if our own excesses may finish us off much sooner.

Our galaxy, the Milky Way, contains about a hundred billion stars, ranging in mass from a tiny proportion of the mass of the sun to a hundred times its mass. That's only our galaxy. There are billions of galaxies in the observable universe. But here's the twist in the story. Though we are a microscopic dot in a tiny corner of a small galaxy in a universe containing billions of galaxies, it is on this dot that the universe has become conscious and has started asking itself questions about its own existence. That's the mystery captured in the final phrase of Primo Levi's poem: 'and this hand that writes'. Very late in the day, we have appeared and started wondering about where it all came from and what it all means. Maybe there are other creatures out there in the universe who are also wondering about it. Some scientists believe that this is possible, maybe even likely. So far, we haven't found the evidence. Not that this has stopped artists imagining the existence of other forms of life on galaxies 'far, far away', to quote the opening sequence of the movie *Star Wars*.

What I can't fathom is where it all came from. That's because I can't follow the answers of those who know more about these things than I do. And it's because, as Kuhn has already warned me, their answers keep changing. I can remember when some of them thought the universe never had a beginning because there had never been a time when it wasn't here. This was called the 'steady state' theory. But it did not answer my naive question either: supposing it *had* always been here, how did it happen always to have been here? I know this is considered a silly question. Stephen Hawking said it was like asking what was north of the north pole. Even so, I can't help asking it. Where did it come from and how did it get here?

The answer on offer today seems to suggest that the universe did indeed have a beginning, which they call the Big Bang, though some claim the originating event was more like a Big Exhalation than a Big Bang. It was a puff that in a trillionth of a trillionth of a second expanded the primordial balloon into a universe of unimaginable extent. And we are told that billions of years after that initial expulsion of energy it continues to expand. Some scientists offer an even softer analogy than the Big Puff. They prefer to think of the blooming of a flower, something that gives rise to beauty and order.

I'm not sure about the puffing or blooming analogies. The history of the universe has always involved explosions and collisions and destruction, though there is undoubtedly a pitiless, flowering beauty in the spectacle. Maybe we should think of it as the Big Fuse or the spark that blew up the munitions dump. Whatever analogies we use, my question still stands: how come? To which they now offer a different answer, which they call a 'singularity', a point of infinite density and gravity (infinitely smaller than the dot above the *i*) in which there was neither time nor space – that blew up

> . . . and every change began.
> Even now the thin echo of this one reverse
>   catastrophe
> Resounds from the farthest reaches.
> From that one spasm everything was born . . .

. . . to quote Primo Levi again.[4] Maybe it's my confusion speaking, but that sounds as question-begging as the answer theologians give to my question 'How come?' The alternative to 'We Don't and May Never Know' is the infinite regress of proposing causes that beg the question of their own causality: OK, we reply, but what caused this cause? Theism tries to put a ledge on this infinite regress by asserting the *necessary* existence of an Uncaused Cause or a Self-Existent Something from which everything else flowed. This is sometimes called *aseity* from the Latin *a/from* and *se/self*, which we might translate as *in-itself-ness*, a reality that contains within itself the cause of its own existence. I'll come back to that story several times in this book, but at this moment it feels more like therapy than causality to me. Or as much therapy as causality: the need to say something rather than admit there is nothing to say. It works if you can will yourself to believe that it actually provides an answer to the problem of existence rather than postponing one. Let me hasten to add that I don't fault anyone for choosing it. It is one of the stories we tell ourselves to give meaning to our lives and stop us going mad. It's just that, for some of us, it no longer serves that purpose. Emily Dickinson got it when she said that for some of us,

> Narcotics cannot still the Tooth
> That nibbles at the soul.[5]

Let me say again that I am not trying to prove or disprove anything in this book, or to grade the theories we keep arriving at to explain ourselves. I am tired of the persuasion game, the dominant-story story and the loud shouting that goes with it. If you are so sure of your story why do you have to make so much noise about it? Why not cleave to it quietly and possess your soul in peace and leave others to their own stories? Haven't you heard that 'Supreme conviction is a self-cure for an infestation of doubts'?[6] Not that I am wanting you to abandon your story or ditch your paradigm. If it works for you, good: live by it. Remember that none of us sees things cleanly as *they* are; only as *we* are; from where we stand; our particular perspective. And that includes much we don't and probably can never know about ourselves and the unconscious forces that drive us.

Anyway, at the moment I am just looking around, trying to figure out where *I* am and how I see things so that I can find the story I want to live by. Whether it happened with a bang, a spark, or a sigh, what I see is a universe that may exist in its own right, uncaused. Or it may have been caused by another reality that was itself uncaused. Either way I am stuck with some version of in-itself-ness, *aseity.* It makes me uncomfortable. But who says my comfort has anything to do with it? Let's move on to look at some of the stories we've told ourselves about where *we* came from and how we got here.

II

WHERE WE CAME FROM

I'm told that a number of factors – directed or un-directed, intended or fortuitous – combined to form the ingredients that started our long journey to where we are today. I have already mentioned the role the sun played in bringing our little planet to life. A tiny shift in the orbit of the earth round the sun and life would never have emerged. A little closer to the sun, it would have been too hot. A little further away, it would have been too cold. Given the precision of that orbital positioning, chemistry seems to have done the rest. Early in our planet's life, the atmosphere was composed of gases in concentrations that would poison most organisms today. Poured from erupting volcanoes, the atmosphere was a mix of methane, ammonia, nitrogen, carbon dioxide and other gases. Earth was dark with clouds that poured down rain to feed the shallow, emerging seas.

Some scientists speculate that what happened next was that a combination of powerful natural forces, such as sunlight, geothermal heat, radioactivity and lighting, provided the critical jolts of energy that made the chemical reactions possible – a bit like the jolt that brought the monster to life in the Frankenstein story. Over billions of years these ingredients formed and reformed into count-less random combinations. And the primal gene was a product of this roulette.

A gene is life's way of remembering how to perpetuate itself. Genes are sections of DNA (deoxyribonucleic acid) that are contained in the chromosomes that are passed on from our parents at conception. The geneticist Marcus Pembrey offered a helpful analogy to explain the relation-ship between genes, DNA and chromosomes. He compared a chromosome to one of those old audio cassettes we used before new technologies banished them to the museum, with DNA the tape inside the cassette and genes the songs on the tape. Genes are not separate from DNA; they are a part of it in the same way that a song was an integral part of the tape inside one of those old cassettes.[1] Anyway, the story goes that there was a moment when the primal gene achieved self-replication. It was the beginning of life in that toxic, primordial sea.

Here's another twist in the story. We didn't know anything about DNA till it was discovered, almost acci-dentally, by a Swiss chemist called Johann Friedrich Miescher in the 1860s. A century later, its beautiful double helix or twisted ladder structure was discovered by two English scientists, James Watson and Francis Crick, in 1953. So, if I had been writing this in 1850, I would not have known of the existence of DNA. And if I had been writing in 1950, I wouldn't have had in my mind the beautiful picture of its structure. DNA was there, of course, begin-ning to do its thing in the lifeless saline seas of the young Planet Earth more than three billion years ago. But we didn't know any of that till not that long ago. Whatever it was and whatever it looked like, at some point the animated result of all these chemical processes heaved itself onto dry land and began its long crawl towards us. It was a slow process, but we had no idea how slow till 1859, when Charles Darwin published his revolutionary book, *On The Origin of Species by Means of Natural Selection.* The creatures that populated our planet had not arrived on the scene fully formed, as we had once imagined. They were the result of glacially slow processes of adaptation to the natural environment that enabled organisms to inherit and pass on characteristics that increased their ability to survive and flourish. Inevitably, Darwin's theory was reduced to the slogan 'Survival of the Fittest', and it captures the central idea. Billions of years after the primal gene had achieved the ability to replicate itself, it evolved into us, and we emerged grunting out of the mist. Here's how the timeline is said to have gone.

What we call *'Homo sapiens',* our clear and obvious ancestor, appeared around 195,000 years ago. I am told we started speaking around 150,000 years ago. With words came ideas and the stories they provoked. And wondering about what happened to people when they died may have been what got it started. We know that at some point in time, rather than leaving them to decompose where they dropped, our ancestors started burying their dead. This would suggest that it was death that got them thinking. What they noticed about the dead was that something that used to happen in them had stopped happening. They no longer *breathed.* It would have been a small step to associate the act of breathing with the idea of something dwelling within yet separate from the physical body that gave it life.

From their observation of breathing or blowing may have come the idea of an invisible entity that inhabited the body for a time and left it at death. Later they would use the Greek word *psyche* or the Latin word *spiritus,* both from verbs meaning to breathe or blow, to describe this entity. Their own experience of their own nature might have contributed something to this idea of a self within but somehow independent of the body. After all, did they not in some sense transcend themselves through their own minds? Were they not a self that thought and wondered and sometimes felt sad? And was it not strange that they could observe themselves as if they were, in some sense, *another*? As these disturbing realisations flickered in their minds, the experience of duality was emerging in human consciousness.

In his literary memoir, *Possessed by Memory: The Inward Light of Criticism*, Harold Bloom coined a difficult phrase to capture this disconcerting human experience: 'self-otherseeing'. It needs explaining. Think of the way you look at others and what you are seeing when you do it. You are seeing other *selves* in all their mystery and separateness. What they do or say may shock, intrigue or outrage you. It may puzzle you. It may stun you into incomprehension or even hatred. *Othering* can cause all these reactions in the observing self. But what if the person you are 'otherseeing' is *yourself*? 'Self-otherseeing' is not seeing yourself as others see you. It is seeing yourself as '*the other*'. Even being baffled or repelled by what you 'self-see'.[2]

This experience of self-transcendence may have triggered the idea of God or gods in early human thinking. After all, if the self could other-see itself, be together and apart from itself at the same time, why could this not be true of the Spirit that inheres in and transcends the universe at one and the same time? It is important to remind ourselves that this would not have occurred to them as an *argument* in favour of transcendence, but as an experience of self-transcendence intuitively projected onto the universe. Later we'll discover that it still works that way for many. No argument is offered, because none is needed. The experience of transcendence is self-authenticating. Which is why assertions of its presence can infuriate those who insist on other ways of explaining it. And it is also why their fury makes no difference.

To go back to these early thinkers: if there was such an other-self, such an entity – however they defined it – where did it go at death? One story was that it went back to that transcendent world, the spirit world, the flipside of the one we inhabited on earth. What we discover of early funeral rites supports that view, though all our distant forebears left us are silent traces of what they might have been thinking. Literature wasn't invented till 4,000 years ago, so our ancestors couldn't leave their thoughts or compose their stories in a form we can read and use today.[3] They did leave clues about what they were thinking at the time, but clues have to be interpreted.

From about 130,000 BCE we find evidence of a vague kind of religious belief in the way our ancestors buried their dead. Food, tools and ornaments were placed in graves, suggesting a belief that the dead travelled on to some kind of afterlife and needed to be equipped for the journey. Another significant practice was the painting of the bodies of the dead with red ochre, maybe to convey the idea of blood or continuing life. This was discovered in one of the oldest known burials, of a mother and child at Qafzeh in Israel sometime around 100,000 BCE. The same practice was found a world away in Australia in 42,000 BCE at Lake Mungo, where the body was also covered in red ochre.

Painting the dead may mark the emergence of one of humanity's most useful storytelling devices. We call it 'symbolic thinking', which is a shorthand way of communicating complicated ideas. As with many other useful words in our vocabulary, 'symbol' comes from the Greek. It's a verb with a prefix: *sum-ballein*. It means to bring together things that had been broken apart, the way you might glue or re-join the bits of a broken plate. A *symbol* became something that stood for or represented something else. It made us re-member or re-call something else. The role of the bread and wine in the Christian Eucharist is a good example. It symbolises or *re-presents* Jesus Christ. A national flag is another example. If we catch a glimpse of the Stars and Stripes, it immediately calls to mind the United States of America. It symbolises or makes present in our minds the idea of that vast nation.

The American philosopher Arthur Danto developed a closely related idea to capture another human compulsion. He described the human animal, in a Latin phrase, as an '*ens representans*', a being that represents or repeats its experience of life back to itself, picturing it, telling its story, sym-bolising it, re-presenting it. Give children crayons and paper, and they'll draw their mummy and daddy and the cat on the mat before the fire. Listen to people in the pub after work and they'll be telling their day over again to their friends. Artists possess this urge for re-presentation to an obsessional degree. Novelists rehearse the complexities of the human condition in a form many of us constantly return to. The best of them don't tell us *about* whatever they are describing; they make it present to us. Here's an example. This is a poet writing about the experience of reading Tolstoy.

If I Could Write Like Tolstoy

you'd see a man
dying in a field with a flagstaff still in his hands.

I'd take you close until you saw the grass
blowing around his head, and his eyes

looking up at the white sky. I'd show you
a pale-faced Tsar on a horse under a tree,

breath from its nostrils, creases in gloved fingers
pulling at the reins, perhaps hoof marks in the mud

as he jumps the ditch at the end of the field.
I'd show you men walking down a road,

one of them shouting to the others to get off it.
You'd hear the ice crack as they slipped down the
    bank

to join him, bringing their horses with them. You'd
    feel

the blood coming out of the back of someone's
    head

warm for a moment, before it touched the snow.
I'd show you a dead man come back to life.

Then I'd make you wait – for pages and pages –
before you saw him go to his window

and look at how the moon turns half a row
of trees silver, leaves the other half black.[4]

Painters are also compulsive reflectors of what is presented
to them in life. Cézanne said the landscape *thought* itself
in him. And some of us can't stop wondering if the
universe might not be thinking itself in us.

But art does more than record and reflect the tumultuous
realities that present themselves to our senses, or to wonder
at them and impose patterns of meaning upon them. It
is also a way of marking our brief moment on earth before
we hurtle into the past, like the famous graffiti 'Kilroy Was
Here' that American GIs etched onto innumerable sites
in Europe during Second World War. There's a Scottish
painting by David Allan that captures this poignant aspect
of art. Done in 1775, and called *The Origin of Painting*, it
is based on a story by the Roman historian Pliny about a
young Corinthian woman who sketched the outline of the
shadow of her lover on a wall before he went off to war,
so that she would have something to remind her of how
he looked when he went away, possibly never to return.
That's the impulse that prompts lovers to carve their

entwined names onto the trunk of a tree to prove that once *they* were here. And it's the impulse behind the journals kept by writers that enable us to go back into their lives and be moved by how they managed their journey through this fleeting world. They remind us that we are all flitting through a lighted hall towards the great unknown, and some of us try to leave a print or mark of our presence before returning to the dark.

All generations have left behind traces or representations of the world they encountered and the stories they told to make sense of it. Centuries later we examine what they have left behind and try to figure out what they made of their time on earth and what they thought came after. A possible reading of the clues our ancestors left at Qafzeh in Israel 100,000 years ago or at Lake Mungo in Australia 42,000 years ago, is that they saw death as the entrance to another phase of existence, imagined as a version of this one. The red ochre they painted on their dead may be a symbol or representation of that belief. It may be a glimpse of what we call a 'religious' belief, 'religion' being the slippery term we use to suggest the presence or existence of a world or reality beyond this one, with death as the connecting door between them.[5]

Here I want to pause and reflect on the meaning of the words 'religious' and 'religion' that I threw into that sentence. If you can bear to read some of the millions of books that have been written on religion, it is easy to get lost in the claims and counter-claims made by those who are authorities on the subject. When reading experts, it is important to remember Auden again: they are 'silly like us'. We have a duty to read them and acknowledge that they know more about the subject than we do. But we should also remember that, like the rest of us, they suffer from unconscious biases that influence how they interpret the thousands of facts they have accumulated. We shouldn't allow their confident explanations to flatten our own thinking on the subject, as long as we remember that we too are flying blind.

Having written those sentences, I want to pause again. They suggest to me that thinking is more an art than a science, which is why it prompts so many disagreements between us. Or have I just posed a false contrast between them? What is the difference between an art and a science anyway? In art we accept the imperative of creativity, of making something happen *for the first time*. Like the young woman etching the outline of her lover onto that wall in Corinth. In contrast to that making of the *new*, of creating something never done or seen before, science progresses on the basis of revealing or unveiling *what was already there* though hidden from us. A good example was the discovery of the double helix by Watson and Crick in 1953. It had been there for billions of years doing its beautiful thing, though science didn't notice it till a few years ago.

There does seem to be a genuine and important distinction between art and science. But maybe it is not absolute. There is real creativity in great scientists: a feeling for what may be going on out there; an ability to make imaginative guesses that turn out to accord with the nature of reality. Nevertheless, the main activity of science is the uncovering of what has always been there though hidden from us, however the process might have been assisted by the creative imaginations of individual scientists.

Thinking too has elements of both art and science in it. It relies on the gathering of facts. Or, to put it a better way, it isn't *thinking* if it ignores or refuses to acknowledge established facts. It is what the thinker does with the facts that matter. Facts have to be interpreted or assembled into patterns of meaning not understood before. That is what makes thinking more of an art than a science. And it accounts for a difficulty common to both art and thinking: the complexities involved in differences of taste or sensibility rooted in the unconscious factors that determine how we interpret the world that lies before us. Here's an example of what I mean.

I dislike baroque architecture. I prefer gothic. I love the novels of Virginia Woolf. But I am not keen on magic realism, which is why some of the novels of Salman Rushdie don't appeal to me. In other words, I am bringing *myself* to the interpretation of reality and the search for meaning. I am imposing preferences upon it. In fact, I am *creating* rather than uncovering meaning. Which is why decent, intelligent people can look at the same accumulation of facts and come to completely different understandings of their meaning. And it is why the human world is so prodigal and varied and hard to deal with.

World is crazier and more of it than we think,
Incorrigibly plural . . .[6]

Which brings me back to this word 'religion' again. I confess to an uncertainty in how best to deal with it. The most usual and obvious way to understand 'religion' is reflected in the story we started telling ourselves when we began to wonder about what happened to the dead. We wondered if there was Something or Someone out there to which or to whom we were related in a dependent, possibly frightening way. That's probably why ugly stuff went on in primitive religion, including the sacrifice of humans as well as animals. Imagine our earliest ancestors trying to make sense of the world in which they found themselves, as their evolving human intelligence flickered into operation. It has been suggested that they fell into a common human response to the unpredictable and the unknown. You hear a creak in the floorboards outside your bedroom on a dark winter night and immediately identify it as the presence of a burglar and reach for the baseball bat beneath your bed. But it turns out to be the wind rattling the timbers of the old farmhouse in which you live.

This nervous ascription of agency to random events has been described as 'Hyperactive Agency-Detection Disorder', or HADD, and it's not hard to understand how it got going. To the primitive mind trying to figure out what caused the pain and sorrow of human existence, an obvious answer was that a powerful and unpredictable supernatural agency was responsible. It made sense, there-fore, to keep it sweet by offering it gifts and tributes.

In time the sprawling complexities of religious practice got tidied onto another one of those symbols we find useful when talking to ourselves, and we came up with the notion of 'God' as the ultimate meaning or meaner of the universe. The trouble with that way of telling the story is that there are religious stories that do not rely on 'God' as the ultimate source of meaning, such as versions of

Buddhism and mystical versions of Christianity that are wary of the idea of 'God' and see it as a conceptual idol. Better to say 'God' is no-thing than to say 'God' is that-thing. All that admitted, it is hard to get rid of a convenient symbol like 'God' to express the idea that there might be a supernatural agent that caused the universe to come into being, in contrast to the idea that the universe is a fortuitous accident that for a time included us in its thrust towards oblivion.

Which brings me to another twist in the story. There are thinkers who insist on using the word 'religion' for all the stories we tell ourselves about the ultimate meaning of things, even if our story is that there is no ultimate meaning. According to this reading, atheism is also a religion. The word atheists use to describe themselves is the giveaway: *a-theist* or no-god. It's a God term even if it is only a negation-of-God term. The refusal or negation of the Ultimate is itself a story of the Ultimate. If religion is the human quest for meaning, and if we decide there is no meaning or no ultimate meaning, it is still a religious decision, because it is an answer to the religious question, even if it's a negative one. It is the question that is religious, not the different answers it finds.

Statistics may provide us with a clue here. Evidence shows that religious belief and observance are declining rapidly in the West, including the USA, especially among what is called Generation Y, those born between 1980 and the year of the millennium, 70 per cent of whom report themselves as having no religion. But nor are they choosing to join organised versions of atheist humanism. In Britain there are several groups that are articulate, intentional and evangelical in their atheism, yet they remain statistically insignificant as organised entities. In Britain the membership figure in 2019 was 70,000 out of a population of sixty-six million. I don't want to push too much meaning into these statistics, but one reading of them is that an increasing number of people live their lives without answering the religious question in either its theist or atheist forms, because they do not ask the question in the first place.

All those qualifications aside, I am still uneasy with the line of thought that lumps intentional atheists in the same basket as intentional theists as *religious*, because they are both obsessed with questions of meaning. Sometimes I think this is just a way of winding up those atheists who betray a religious or evangelical intensity in promoting their atheism. Why, we might ask, are you so worked up about denying the existence of a transcendent reality whose presence is beyond our capacity to prove or disprove? Are you worried it might actually be out there? There is fun in playing that game. But I don't enjoy it now. One of the things I am trying to suggest in this book is that contradictory stories can honestly be told about the world. I am hoping to find a way of living creatively with these differences. And I think it is ungracious and unnecessary to deny that they exist. To claim that thinkers who claim to be atheists are actually believers in another kind of absolute is childish and insulting.

The disconcerting thing about us is that we can consider the same facts, the same realities, and come to diametrically opposed interpretations of their meaning. We can even reach different conclusions from reading the same science.

What this suggests is that we bring an unavoidable creativity to our interpretations or representations of reality, because thinking is more an art than a science. We also bring our biases and prejudices, so if we are wise and compassionate, we won't reject an art form because it is not to our taste. We just won't buy it for ourselves. Can't we apply that principle more widely? Let me turn now to a chasm of understanding between two ways of thinking about how the world brought us into being and what it thought it was doing when it did, if it was thinking at all.

Theists not only claim that God as its creator is a good explanation for the existence of the *universe*, they also believe God is the best explanation for the precise emergence of the human species within it. Among those who take this view are believing scientists who point to several different levels of support for it. To me the most intriguing part of their argument is the human discovery or invention of mathematics as the instrument that helped humans penetrate the nature, extent and functioning of the physical universe. Mathematicians sit in their studies and do their abstract calculations, which turn out to map closely onto the physical mechanics of the universe. Among other benefits of these abstract calculations is our ability to send astronauts to the moon 240,000 miles away and land a probe on Mars thirty-four million miles away. Closer to home, the satellites orbiting above our heads in space have enabled neurologically incompetent people like me to arrive at their destinations through the use of satellite navigation technology. It turns out that human mathematics is the key that turns the lock that opens the lid on the engine box of the physical universe. How can we account for this symmetry? One explanation is that the physical universe is itself the work of a Mind that our minds are able to connect with and interpret.[7] Like connects with like, deep with deep, mind with Mind.

No matter how we account for it, the correspondence between the human mind and the working of the universe is intriguing. That's why some argue that even though we cannot make direct contact with the mind of the maker, we can connect with it indirectly through its handiwork. It's something like the way critics probe the writings of dead authors to find out what they had been thinking. Direct access to the authors' minds is impossible. What they are in touch with are their effects, the traces they have left, words on paper. And that's how it is with God. We don't encounter *him*. We only discover where he has been or what he has done. The poet R.S. Thomas put it like this:

His are the echoes
We follow, the footprints he has
Just left.[8]

The other intriguing element in the story believing scientists point to is the fine tuning that made our appearance possible, if not inevitable. One version of this explanation is called 'intelligent design', and its proponents even adapt evolutionary theory to fit their argument. The emergence of humans and other living creatures is best explained as the intended result of an intelligent mind, rather than as the happenstance of an unintended and undirected process. The chemistry of the universe was precisely designed to produce us. Called 'anthropic balances', the precise calibrations or fine tuning required to produce us, they claim, were as likely as aiming at a target an inch square on the other side of the universe and hitting it. Impossible odds, so there must have been a plan and a planner.

Those who offer the 'divine planner' story as a solution to the puzzles that beset us do not claim to *prove* the existence of a Creator in this way, but they think it adds support to a belief that may be held on other grounds, as yet another creative human response to the facts in front of us. One conclusion, therefore, is that the 'God' of these arguments is best understood as a human construct, a hypothesis, a calculation. Of course, it may turn out to be inspired guess work, the way scientists suggest a theory to account for the facts they encounter, test it and then decide they were right. Later I'll look at the way believers think the 'God' hypothesis has been verified through direct human experience. But where we are in this story now is that, as a hypothesis, 'God' offers us an elegant solution to the problem of our own appearance in the universe and the fact that our minds seem to be so finely tuned to its workings and dynamics.

On the other or opposite side of the explanatory chasm from the anthropic principle, two replies are offered. The well-mannered response is that there is no need to go outside the universe and identify a supernatural agent to account for our appearance in it, since there are good, entirely natural explanations available. One is that in a multiverse (a universe containing an incalculable, possibly infinite number of universes) every possible combination of factors is likely, including one that will give rise to sentient life. It is a bit like visiting an enormous department store containing every conceivable range of clothing size. We are bound to find a suit that fits us. It just happens to be the case that on our little blue planet we have found ourselves in a galaxy that carries our range.

I am not sure I am quite persuaded by this argument either, as an *argument*. It is plausible, of course. But is it maybe too plausible, as though it is being reached for to avoid having to take the other route, the supernatural route? It may be that, subconsciously, we all settle for explanations we are predisposed to accept, and reject those we are predisposed against. Some minds are clearly hostile to any taint of theism and the department store analogy gives them a plausible alternative. A point in its favour is that it is at least polite in how it makes its case. Not all atheistic arguments have the same level of courtesy. Here's one that is riddled with contempt.

> Why . . . would the shaper of the universe have frittered away thirteen billion years, turning out quadrillions of useless stars, before getting around to the one thing he really cared about, seeing to it that a minuscule minority of earthling vertebrates are washed clean of sin and guaranteed an eternal place in its company?[9]

The sneaky thing about that snort of derision is that it conceals an unexamined assumption, which is that belief in God necessarily implies the Christian salvation story, which is itself a story within a story – and one I'll examine later in this book. All that needs to be said now is that the God hypothesis can be articulated in a thousand ways other than the Christian one, so it's unfair to claim they are the same thing. Why not just shake your head and say to the believers in a divine creator, Sorry, I just don't see it like that? Why the compulsion to have a go at them? Religions are complex systems. Some are drenched in fear and superstition. But some are intellectually sophisticated and deserve an intelligent hearing.

All this recalls Kuhn's point about different ways of looking at the same thing. Or my point about the creativity we all bring to our interpretations of reality. As well as reading stories *out of* what we perceive, we also read stories *into* what we perceive. We see things not as they are but as we are. This happens in religion as well as in science and politics and in almost all human endeavours. The theologian John Hick advised us that 'the forms taken by religious experience are provided by the conceptual equipment of the experiencer'. He quotes the tenth-century Sufi al-Junayd: 'The colour of water is that of its container.' Adding a comment from Ibn al-'Arabi: 'If one knew Junayd's saying, he would not interfere with other men's beliefs, but would perceive God in every form of belief.'[10] I would widen that warning to include all beliefs, including the belief that there is no God to believe in.

A tactic used by experts engaged in conflict resolution is worth reflecting on here. Protagonists are advised to prepare arguments supporting the view with which they most strongly disagree. It's a taxing exercise, which is why we find it difficult to practise and are more comfortable with its opposite, which is hearing our views confirmed and those of our opponents ridiculed – a well-known trope in both religious and political debate. The conflict here is the 'who' or 'what' problem we face. Did some kind of transcendent mind – external to or beyond the mechanics or physics of the natural processes that produced us – cause or intend our existence? Or are we the fortuitous and unintended result of natural processes that aim at nothing and achieve nothing other than the expression of their own being?

Speaking personally, though I admire the intelligence and care that went into each of the responses from the different sides of the explanatory chasm, neither of them absolutely grabs or persuades me. And I suspect my uneasiness is more emotional than intellectual, or as much emotional as intellectual. The arguments offered in support of each conclusion do not *feel* authentic as *arguments* to me. My instinct tells me that each is an intellectualising or rationalising of a position held on other, possibly intuitive grounds. It's as if each side had been originally predisposed to respond in a particular way to the problem posed by our existence and reject other solutions, another example of how we bring ourselves to the table whenever we debate these issues. We genuinely want to see things as *they* are, but we can't help seeing them as *we* are or from where we see them.

Our difficulty is that it is hard to get ourselves out of the way when we are handling these ideas. What we are and where we come from influences how and what we see. That's why we should read the stories others have told or continue to tell with as much tolerance and understanding as we can muster. Theists and atheists – and those who are comfortable in neither slot – should acknowledge that though they may have come to diametrically opposed views, they are responding to the same facts. And they should remember that thinking is a creative act that conjures different meanings from the reality it encounters.

My personal dilemma is that I feel the strength of each of these opposing perspectives, but am able to commit myself permanently to neither. No, that's not it either. It is more that I find myself able to occupy both positions – theist and atheist – at the same time. I wonder if this is an example of what is sometimes called the 'Scottish disjunction' or the 'Caledonian antisyzygy', which is the existence of opposing or competing polarities in the same entity. In the case of Scotland, it seems to have been a psychological response to our long and turbulent love/hate relationship with England, a relationship that became co-dependent but hardly co-equal with the Union of Parliaments in 1707.

If England was Scotland's original sin, the source of our unease with ourselves, I experienced the complexity of the relationship with particular force because I was part English and resented it. When I was growing up in the Vale of Leven, I regretted not having a Scottish surname like those of my school friends. My father's mother was a Buchanan, a Scot, but his father was a Holloway, an Englishman, so I was stuck with that name. There were no Holloways in those books about the Scottish clans I used to pore over in the local library. But there were plenty of Buchanans.

Another source of ambivalence was my faith tradition. I belonged to the Scottish Episcopal Church, 'the English Kirk' to everyone in the town I lived in. You could tell people till you were blue in the face that Scottish

Episcopalians were an authentic Scottish community that was outlawed for its loyalty to the Stuart cause in the Jacobite rebellions, but it made no difference. We were 'the English church, the lairds' church, the church the toffs went to'.

I left Scotland at fourteen to study for the priesthood. In England. And a new kind of ambivalence emerged, this time about sounding too Scottish. I discovered that the English quite liked the Scots, in an amused, sometimes patronising way. The fact that we were not a problem to them only made our problem with them more frustrating. I was picking up something else, the difference in the way Scotland and England did religion. There was a sense in which the English took it less seriously, maybe even less grimly, than we did north of the border. And while I belonged to the Anglican theological tradition, with its feel for balance and compromise, part of me admired the fierceness of the Scottish style and its contempt for the half-hearted. Our history was characterised by schisms, disruptions and vehement disagreements. Even the way we spoke could feel like a punch in the face. Our much bigger neighbour to the south wasn't to blame for this, but she did exert an immense gravitational pull that had a distorting effect on our sense of ourselves and how we expressed it.

I was beginning to experience the range and oppositions of human experience in politics and religion, and how difficult it was to take a side and stay there permanently. From time to time I affected a side, took a position. But there was usually a kind of posturing involved, an assuming of an attitude. No sooner did I affect the Cavalier or the Jacobite than I began to feel the moral force of the

Roundhead or the Covenanter. What was happening in me was an interiorising of the dualities that seem to be intrinsic to the human condition, another form of the disjunction or antisyzygy that characterises actual human experience. I found its best expression in the words of the historian Thomas Babington Macaulay, the son of an Anglicised Scottish father and an English mother. Macaulay believed that the disjunctions that afflicted us were intrinsic to the human condition and there was no permanent escape from them. They had their origin

> . . . in diversities of temper, of understanding, and of interest, which are found in all societies, and which will be found till the human mind ceases to be drawn in opposite directions by the charm of habit and by the charm of novelty . . . Everywhere there is a class of men who cling with fondness to whatever is ancient, and who, even when convinced with overpowering reasons that innovation would be beneficial, consent to it with many misgivings and forebodings. We find also everywhere another class of men sanguine in hope, bold in speculation, always pressing forward, quick to discern the imperfections of whatever exists, disposed to think lightly of the risks and inconveniences which attend improvements, and disposed to give every change credit for being an improvement. In the sentiments of both classes there is something to approve. But of both the best specimens will be found not far from the common frontier. The extreme section of one class consists of bigoted dotards; the extreme section of the other consists of shallow and reckless empirics.[11]

Looking back, I wonder if the experiences that formed my later attitudes towards human conflict weren't being established subconsciously back then before I was capable of interpreting them or even knowing they were happening. It was like being on Macaulay's common frontier, and the compulsion was to look both ways. Is there something about people who live on a frontier that renders them incapable of the decisive either/or and disposes them towards the indefinite both/and? I am not claiming that this is a universal Scottish characteristic – the opposite, the permanently adversarial posture can also result – but it does seem to be the case that many Scots do possess it or are possessed by it. They certainly write about it a lot, often in poetry. Here's the poet Robert Crawford.

> When you are faced with two alternatives
> Choose both. And should they put you to the test,
> Tick every box. Nothing is ever single.
> A seed's a tree's a ship's a constellation.
> Nail your true colours to this branching mast.[12]

That reminds me of Louis MacNeice's description of the world as *incorrigibly plural*. Come to think of it, he also was a man of the frontier, a border man, Anglo-Irish. None of this was ever just about the Anglo-Scots or the Anglo-Irish or any other tribe living across an awkward frontier. But it was the beginning of my personal experience of what is humanity's biggest problem, wherever it finds itself. *Us.*

PART II

STORIES WE TOLD
OURSELVES BEFORE WE
KNEW THE STORIES
SCIENCE TOLD US ABOUT
OURSELVES

III

WHY WE ARE A PROBLEM

Whenever in the past I was promoting a confident theism, I did it with a level of discomfort that was more professional than personal. The issue of 'God' or 'No God' can be vexing for anyone to deal with, but it becomes tougher if you find yourself as a professional in one of the systems that promotes a particular version or understanding of God. Let me continue my analogy with politics.

Some of us have a settled and lifelong interest in politics. Some have no interest at all and don't even bother to vote. They are a bit like those people who show no interest in religion or questions of meaning and live their lives indifferent to the movements around them that pursue those concerns. Just as those interested in religion may become professional clergy, so those interested in politics may become professional politicians. In both cases it is the professionalism that is the game-changer. Though politics is as shifting and uncertain a practice as religion, if you become a parliamentarian you have to commit yourself to the manifesto your party has adopted, usually somewhere along a spectrum that ranges, in Macaulay's language, from reckless empiricism at one end to ignorant bigotry at the other. Or to put it in more temperate language, between those who find change and experiment seductive and those who find it repellent, the old tension between the charm of novelty and the charm of habit.

But what happens if you change your mind and shift along the spectrum in a different direction from your party's official position? Such shifts can be painful, leading to the parting of friends and the severing of relationships, even if you are only an amateur in the political game and watch it from the sidelines. They are much tougher if you are a professional representative of a party in parliament. Most political parties are what they call broad churches or coalitions that manage to operate along a wide section of the spectrum, with their more radical elements at the outer edges. Even so, some parliamentarians become so uncomfortable with their party's line that they cross the floor and join the other side. It is always a painful business that can lead to accusations of treason or apostasy. There are commentators who believe that the party system itself is intrinsically flawed, because it boxes people into the defence of ideas they may no longer believe in. The problem is deeper than that, and the word 'believe' is the giveaway.

It is very common to hear politicians, when debating the issues of the day, tell us they *believe* in this or that solution to some problem or crisis they are confronting. The trouble with that particular verb is that while it gives us information about the psychological state of the speaker, it gives us no useful information about the matter that is being debated or believed in. A good example was what Prime Minister Tony Blair called his masochism strategy during the prelude to the Iraq War in 2003. He toured the country, bravely confronting opponents of his determination to take the UK into the US-led invasion of a faraway country that seemed to have nothing to do with our own interests or security. There was no doubt of his sincerity. He burned with it. He constantly told his audiences how strongly he believed in what he was planning to do. Among the things he believed in was the existence of weapons of mass destruction in Iraq that were pointed in our direction. We were told by others at the time, some of them with knowledge of the issue rather than beliefs, that there was little if any evidence that they existed. We went to war anyway, on the basis of the Prime Minister's passionate beliefs. No weapons of mass destruction were found, but the intervention provoked an avalanche of events that will surge indefinitely into the future, determining the lives of populations as yet unborn.

A similar dynamic is at work in Britain as I write this in 2019. The disagreement is over Britain's relationship with the European Union and whether or not we should break from it or Brexit. Again, it is a competition between conflicting belief systems, each of them passionately and sincerely held, each with its cadre of experts who offer facts in support of their team's beliefs. But the passion comes from the beliefs not the facts. Facts always have to be interpreted, especially if they are the consequence of complicated human interventions stretching over many years. And they can look very different from the opposite sides of the divides we find ourselves shouting across. This is why human history is so insistently tragic, and why so many of our disagreements seem beyond reconciliation.

Our problem is that, as well as possessing a capacity for reason and reflection, we are also a highly suggestible species, prone to crazes, panics, conspiracy theories and other psychological spasms: in short, beliefs. Beliefs, like communicable diseases, are highly infectious. I can remember the craze for the belief that the intricate crop circles that started to appear in fields in East and West Lothian in the late twentieth and early twenty-first centuries were the work of Unidentified Flying Objects from outer space or other paranormal agencies. Most of them turned out to be hoaxes, or to be consistent with human causation, but that made little difference to the true believers at the time. Beliefs can be negative as well as positive. They can be *disbeliefs* in events amply proved to have happened, using reliable methods of verification, as well as the testimony of thousands of eyewitnesses. Examples are those Holocaust deniers who disbelieve, contrary to all the evidence, that six million Jews were ever exterminated in Nazi Germany in the 1940s; or those who believe that the moon landing of 1969, the world's most universally recorded and publicised event, never happened. Disbeliefs of this sort are as hard to dislodge as their polar opposites.

We are all prone to these lapses and indecisions and spasms of irrationality. Even the exact detail of events we genuinely witnessed can elude us. Meyerhold, the Russian theatre director, used to tell a story from his days as a law student at Moscow University. A professor would arrange for a powerful thug to rush into the classroom in the middle of a lecture. There would be a fight, the police would be called and the troublemaker removed. Then the students would be asked to recount what had happened. Each would tell a different story; some would even insist that there had been not one thug but two. Hence, the professor would explain, the Russian saying: 'He lies like an eyewitness.'[1]

The trouble with dwelling on humanity's capacity for error and psychological intoxication is that it can paralyse the will to action in thoughtful people and immobilise them in the face of the decisions they have to take if they are to play their part in the human historical struggle. If we know we are so prone to error and misjudgement, how can we ever find the will to engage in human affairs? The challenge is to acknowledge our capacity for error without letting it paralyse the will to action. All our judgements should be hedged against the possibility that we may be wrong. They should be tinged with a flavour of provisionality, a sense of experiment rather than certainty. We'll remember how often we changed our minds in the past, so we'll constantly engage in acts of self-examination and submit ourselves to the interrogation of others. In a letter written from prison in December 1929, the Italian Marxist Antonio Gramsci described the dialectic I am reaching for when he said we should practise pessimism of the intellect and optimism of the will, a disjunction that will only work if both ends of the dialectic stay in touch with each other. We will certainly choose to act, but we'll hold the necessary act in tension with the possibility that we may be mistaken as we perform it. This radical realism about ourselves should not depress us, it should encourage and cheer us. After all it was realism about ourselves that helped us fumble our way towards the practice of representative democracy, with its built-in structures of opposition and challenge to government. Democracy is built on a pessimistic understanding of human nature and a consequent mistrust of those with power over us. Tony Benn used to ask of those in positions of power, how do we get rid of you when the time comes? That is why systems of accountability and reversal should be built into all our power relations, even the most intimate.

More difficult, but just as essential, is the need to build the same systems of challenge and reversal into our own thinking. We must live with the knowledge that we may be wrong about things, and that we too are capable of lying like an eyewitness, even if it is only to ourselves. Humour is a key ingredient here. Humour, especially ironic humour, is the best way of puncturing human arrogance. And it is most useful when wielded by the self against the self. We might say, therefore, that the sanest guide through the turbulence and hatred of human politics is a humorous and self-deprecating pessimism.

The same balance should be struggled for in religion and its endemic controversies, but it is rarely achieved, because faith systems are usually authoritarian in their practice and self-definition and, with one or two exceptions, they tend to believe that their own version is the perfect and final word on the subject. Most of them were formed to promote a fixed belief in an ultimate reality whose existence, though uncertain, they are never permitted to doubt. That is why in their institutional character, faith communities rarely engage openly in what has been one of humanity's most intractable disagreements. Instead they proclaim or announce a final solution to the matter that is designed to close the argument down. These definitive proclamations usually take the form of statements of belief called 'creeds', from the Latin for believe. But, as in political manifestos, they too easily switch from expressions of belief to defiant statements of fact. That's where their danger lies.

A classic example of the genre is a long, brutally assertive creed, composed in the late fifth century CE, which begins, '*Quicumque vult salus esse*' or 'Whosoever would be saved'. It was meant to put a stop to a debate in the Western Church that was not so much about the *existence* of God as about God's *nature* or how God *was* God. Was God Single and Alone? Was God *One*, as Islam would later proclaim with passionate certainty? Or was there *communion* or *relationship* in God, something analogous to *family*? The 'Quicumque Vult' stated categorically that God was both Single *and* In Communion with Itself, One *and* Three. But the 'Quicumque Vult' did more than assert the complicated metaphysical arithmetic of the Holy Trinity. Its authors told the faithful that this is what God was really, really like, and if they did not get with the idea, '*without doubt they would perish everlastingly*'.

I have to pause here and reflect on the monstrousness of the words I have just quoted: *without doubt they would perish everlastingly*. And not for anything they *did*. Not for their complicity in the moral horrors that stain human history. Not for humanity's many genocides. Not for persecuting people of a different colour or religion. Not for their pitiless abuse of children, Ivan Karamazov's deepest sorrow. Not for any of that. Not for anything *done*. Instead, damned for refusing to or not being able to hold a particular proposition or sequence of words in their heads. For not being in possession of whatever the perfect God *idea* is. Or for not having a clue what it means. Owner of the saving knowledge myself, I might announce to you: 'The nature of the Ultimate Uncreated Self-Existent One is revealed in the Multitudinous Self-Referential Circularity of its own In-ness and utter lack of Out-ness. And unless you wholeheartedly assent and pledge yourself to the truth of this self-evidencing certainty *YOU WILL BURN IN HELL FOR EVER!*

It is significant that the 'Quicumque Vult' is rarely recited in Christian worship nowadays, though it has never been officially repudiated. Instead, it has been banished to that attic of embarrassing relics called 'Historical Documents of the Church', which is found at the back of modern versions of *The Book of Common Prayer*, much in the way wealthy Victorians parked their insane relatives in the local bedlam or asylum. Out of the way, but never entirely out of mind.

Where does it come from, this notion that a form of words held in our heads can either save us or kill us? Or that a thought or theory can damn or redeem us? The philosopher Roger Scruton – a religious believer himself – has observed that, 'When a system of belief starts to persecute those who do not accept it, we know – or ought to know – that it is a pseudo-science.'[2] Both politics and religion, human arts that are intrinsically shifting and uncertain because they are the way we channel our hopes, fears and insecurities, possess an ungovernable urge to turn themselves into infallible systems of knowledge – pseudo-sciences in Scruton's language – against which they can then measure the fidelity of their adherents and punish them for their lapses. Another word for this frantic assumption of certainty is what the ancient world called 'Gnosticism', from the Greek word for knowledge – in Latin '*Scientia*', that science thing again – which is the belief that salvation from the tumults and sorrows of this troubled world can be achieved by acquiring and wielding a special kind of know-how, a knowledge that alone can save.[3]

There is, of course, such a thing as saving knowledge. Knowing how to perform cardiopulmonary resuscitation on someone who has stopped breathing is a good example. Or how to apply an Epipen to someone suffering from anaphylactic shock. Or how to land a Jumbo jet when one of its engines fails. These are all examples of knowledge that saves lives. But there's nothing secret or mystical about the knowledge applied in these situations. It is out there to be learned or acquired with attention and hard work.

The saving knowledge promoted by gnostic systems is different. It is *secret*, known only to its adepts and initiates. In the philosophies of the ancient world it was achieved through the practice of a form of contemplation that opened the aspirant to its in-flowing from its source in the divine. In modern secular cultures the mystical or supernatural side of Gnosticism may have become less explicit, but it is still there, though cloaked in a different vocabulary. In essence, it is the belief that the human world is profoundly damaged and can only be repaired by those who possess the secret which alone can heal it. In its twentieth-century political versions, Roger Scruton has described it not as in the antisyzygy of Gramsci's pessimism of the intellect and optimism of the will, but as its polar opposite, a unidirectional form of what he calls 'unscrupulous optimism'. He says it is based on the belief that 'the difficulties and disorders of humankind can be overcome by some large-scale adjustment: it suffices to devise a new arrangement, a new system, and people will be released from their temporary prison into a realm of success.'[4]

It is *optimistic*, because it believes it knows exactly how to fix the problems of the human community – and how to fix them for ever. It is *unscrupulous*, because of the cheerful way it is prepared to sacrifice the lives of any who get in the way of its ultimate self-realisation. It was seen at work in the purges and pogroms of Soviet Communism in the twentieth century. A current example is China's re-education camp programme, which is designed to purge the minds of recalcitrant Muslims of their reactionary religious ideas and implant the saving knowledge of Leninist Communism into their brains. A more obviously religious version of unscrupulous optimism in our own time is the attempt by Isis to establish the perfect Islamic Caliphate in the Middle East, no matter the slaughter required to achieve it. What always hypnotises the gnostic mind is the idea that it is in possession of the secret formula that has eluded every other human community in history: how to achieve and maintain the perfect society. And its most dominant characteristic is its absolute rejection of dissent.

If you resist, without doubt you will perish everlastingly is always the motto of these eschatologists with their final solutions to the human problem and their unscrupulous pursuit of it. That is why, whatever form they take in history, whether secular or religious, they always establish regiments of thought police to root out those who refuse to accept the saving knowledge that is destined to transform the world, in order either to re-educate them or to eliminate them. In its religious manifestations, the ultimate gulags may be in hell rather than in Siberia or Mesopotamia, but the methods are the same. Its inquisitors torture and interrogate dissenters in the name of their supernatural version of whatever their final solution is. A searing example from religious history is the story of Giordano Bruno, an Italian free-thinker who anticipated many of the ideas of modern science, and in the process clearly contradicted a literalist reading of the creation narrative in the Bible. Arrested by the secret police of the Roman Catholic Church, known as the 'Holy Office', he was put through eight years of trials and was finally burned alive on the Campo de' Fiori in Rome in 1600 for holding a 'wrong' idea in his head, proving just how dangerous it is in the absolute systems of gnostic societies to think for yourself – or to think at all.[5]

The truth behind all the cruelties that stain our history in both their religious and political forms is the fact that we humans are damaged and deeply flawed creatures, thinking animals who spend their lives trying to figure themselves out. The lie in our souls is the belief that there is a miracle cure for our condition out there somewhere, whether political or religious, and if we can but find it and ruthlessly apply it, we'll blow all our troubles away. All these systems ignore the fact that we are the virus we suffer from, and we carry it with us into all these perfect societies. Once you accept the incurable nature of human-ity's disease, it inoculates you against all absolute systems and their ruthless optimists with daggers up their sleeves. Here's Joan Didion again:

> . . . the ambiguity of belonging to a generation distrustful of political highs, the historical irrelevancy of growing up convinced that the heart of darkness lay not in some error of social organization but in man's own blood. If man was bound to err, then any social organization was bound to be in error. It was a premise which still seems to me accurate enough, but one which robbed us early of a certain capacity for surprise.[6]

There are, of course, wise ways of living with this pessi-mistic diagnosis of the human condition. There's another linguistic surprise, '*dia-gnosis*'. This time it's a friend and helper. It's from the Greek *dia* (apart) and *gignoskein* (recog-nise or know). That is, to know in the sense of to discern, to figure out, to separate the real from the phoney. Intriguing how the words we use are sometimes wiser than we are, as is the case here . . .

But how do we learn to acknowledge the impulses and mis-directions of our flawed nature? The first step is to own and admit them. Only then can we build floodwalls to moderate and manage our destructive urges. Our slow and never finished struggle towards systems of represent-ative democracy is an example of realism about ourselves. As was the way civilised societies moved from the vendetta and other methods of personal revenge against offence towards state-controlled systems of criminal justice. We know from our own literary fictions how imperfect even those so-called solutions turned out to be. Most thrillers and detective stories involve corrupt police officers in the pay of the criminals they are supposed to protect us from. We know there is no permanent cure for our condition. We are the disease we suffer from, and we carry it with us into all the promised lands we trek towards.

Promised lands . . .

Readers will get the religious echo here from the story of the Israelites' escape from slavery in Egypt into the promised land of peace and plenty. Except it didn't turn out like that for them either. Promised lands never do. History reminds us that our only paradises are lost paradises, the ones that never lasted, the ones in all those stories about golden ages that never were. That's why it is still useful to learn how to read those old religious stories we told ourselves back then before we knew the story modern science told us about who we are and where we came from. Stories about our wanderings in search of that abiding place that haunts our imagination. Stories about the monsters we met and defeated as we made our way. And were defeated by, again and again. Stories that describe the good place we found, round the next bend in the river where the cottonwoods grew. And ruined, because we brought ourselves and our discontents with us into the haven we longed for.

Or maybe it is more important not to *misread* these old stories. Or not to misread them *wilfully*. Maybe it is the pain of their meaning we run from because they also tell us there is no escape from ourselves. That's what we'll find when we take a look at some of them in the next chapter and try to explore their meaning for us today. We'll have to be careful *how* we read them, or what we read into them. We know from our own history how professional religious teachers have misused them in the past and keep on misusing them today.

Which brings us back to Scruton's warning about turning our beliefs into pseudo-sciences. We find it painful to accept that the human condition is a rolling crisis we can learn to manage wisely but from which we can never escape. And because we cannot bear the thought of the permanence of our imperfections, we turn gratefully to professional fixers – religious and political – who promise us salvation *if we will put ourselves into their hands and swallow their prescriptions for what ails us.* They present themselves as saviours with a cure for our condition, but they always end by intensifying rather than healing the disease we suffer from. That's why we should read history and learn from it not to expect too much from humankind. Its great set-pieces are all crowd scenes. Multitudes, eyes shining with faith and longing, going into the wilderness to hear the latest prophet, eager to place themselves completely under his direction.

Multitudes, multitudes, in the valley of decision!
For the day of the Lord is near in the valley
    of decision.[7]

Our history is littered with the victims of these cruel optimists and the ruins of the utopias they built to cure us of ourselves. It is also bristling with the revenge we took upon those who denied our dreams and interrupted their fulfilment. That is certainly the story of the twentieth century, two thirds of which I lived through, having been born in 1933, the year Hitler became chancellor of Germany. The devastating thing about the history of my century is how it confirms a pessimistic reading of human nature. One of the lessons it teaches is that everything in human affairs is connected to everything else. That's why the science writer Carl Sagan told us that if we wanted to make an apple pie from scratch we'd first have to invent the universe. And why my history tutor claimed it would be possible to trace the causes of the First World War in 1914 to the building of the Great Wall of China in the seventh century BCE. He meant that actions have consequences that reverberate in widening circles, far beyond the originating act and far into the distant future. An example is how what they thought of as the end of the First World War in 1918 was only another surge in the pitiless flow of events. W.B. Yeats wrote a poem in 1920, as the First World War continued itself by other means in the committee rooms of Versailles, in which he used the metaphor of the gyre or spiral to express the interconnectedness of all our actions.

Turning and turning in the widening gyre
The falcon cannot hear the falconer;
Things fall apart; the centre cannot hold;
Mere anarchy is loosed upon the world . . .

And what rough beast, its hour come round at last,
Slouches towards Bethlehem to be born?[8]

Yeats could not have realised it, but the rough beast he prophesied was a German soldier called Adolf Hitler, who had been temporarily blinded at the end of the war and was convalescing in a Pomeranian hospital where he brooded on the humiliation of his people:

> I knew that all was lost. Only fools, liars and criminals could hope for mercy from the enemy. In these nights hatred grew in me, hatred for those responsible for this deed . . . The more I tried to achieve clarity on the monstrous events in this hour, the more the shame of indignation and disgrace burned my brow. What was all the pain in my eyes compared to this misery? In the days that followed, my own fate became known to me . . . I resolved to go into politics.[9]

It turns out that humanity's greatest problem is not knowing how we came to be or even how the universe came up with us, but how we *are*, how we behave, how we act, what we are like, and what, if anything, we can do about it. And we are back to the idea of stories as guides for living. It is here religious stories, if we read them intelligently and not as the script for yet another rescue plan, can be a help. They show us what it is like to be this thinking, feeling, troubled creature, formed by forces it had no control over, wandering in the haunted wood of existence. The artists who composed them did not know the story science now tells us about how the universe brought us forth. Whatever they themselves believed about the origins of the universe, the best way for us to read them today is as art, true fictions that tell us something about ourselves. Read that way, they still have lessons to teach us about how we might become better versions of ourselves. Which is why I want to turn now to some of the most famous stories in religious history, the creation narratives from the Hebrew Bible.

IV

THE CREATION

I am tempted to begin this chapter by advising the reader in advance how to read the old stories I am about to copy out, but it would be a mistake. Or worse than a mistake. Unfair. A sneaky way of smuggling my own perplexities or prejudices into the narrative. All I'll say now is that at the stage in history when the stories I want to explore in this chapter were being written, no one knew what science now tells us about the origins of the universe and our appearance within it, the outlines of which I sketched in the early chapters of this book.

One other fact to register before moving on: once a story is out there, it takes on a life of its own that even its author cannot control. It does its own thing. But it also has things done to it, ways of reading it that are acts of distortion and mutilation, which then become another story that takes on a life of its own. And the river rolls on. I daresay I'll do a bit of distortion myself as I look again at the ancient narratives that provide the substance of this chapter. It'll be hard not to. But mainly what I want to do is *think* about them. Thinking is a creative act that can disclose or discover new meanings in old stories, even if the way they are read departs from the

interpretations of the scholars who have assumed owner-
ship of the material.

A support to the approach I am trying to follow here
was provided by reading Jonathan Rée's vast carnival of a
book, *Witcraft: The Invention of Philosophy in English*. He
notices how professional philosophers have treated the
subject as their exclusive domain, so the history of philosophy becomes the story of their opinions and interactions
with each other over the centuries, which is why so many
people find it such a dry and intimidating subject to grapple
with. Rée comments:

> . . . what we look back on as the inert reality of the past
> was once a myriad of possible futures, to be determined
> by choices that had not yet been made . . . But the histo-
> rians of philosophy have carried on as before, repeating
> familiar stories about the little band of philosophers who
> have become mainstays of modern textbooks . . . they
> have continued to ignore all the other people who have
> tried to understand the world in the light of philosophy
> and who were, as often as not, transformed by the expe-
> rience. Philosophy taught them that notions they had
> always taken for granted might not be valid after all. It
> gave them the courage to ask their own questions about
> how the world works and how they should lead their
> lives. It opened their minds and set them free . . . I hope
> my stories will bring out the ordinariness of philosophy,
> as well as its magnificence and its power to change
> people's lives. And I hope you will end up seeing it as a
> carnival rather than a museum: an unruly parade of free
> spirits, inviting you to join in and make something new.[1]

If philosophy is too important to be left to the philosophers, then that is equally if not more true of religion. If religion is the human quest for meaning, then it is too important to be left to scholars and professionals, both of whom have a tendency to tell us that how they see things is the only possible way to see them. In that spirit, let me turn now to one of the greatest artists in the never-ending carnival of storytelling that is human history, remembering Jonathan Rée's exhortation to have the courage to ask our own questions and find our own meanings. I have chosen two stories from Genesis, the first book of the Hebrew Bible, and they are among the most famous stories ever told. Whatever their original author intended by them, they have become the supreme example of narratives upon which colossal edifices of meaning and interpretation have been erected over the centuries, throwing long shadows into our own day – an example of how stories take on a life of their own once they are out there and go on doing their own thing. This should encourage us to think for ourselves as well and, in Rée's phrase, 'make something new'.

It may be worth noting that there is no universally agreed date for Genesis, though it is usually placed somewhere around the ninth or eighth centuries BCE. Here's the first part of the Genesis story.

In the beginning God created the heavens and the earth. The earth was without form and void, and darkness was upon the face of the deep; and the Spirit of God was moving over the face of the waters. And God said, 'Let there be light'; and there was light. And God saw that the light was good; and God separated the light from the darkness. God called the light Day, and the darkness he called Night. And there was evening and there was morning, one day.

And God said, 'Let there be a firmament in the midst of the waters, and let it separate the waters from the waters.' And God made the firmament and separated the waters which were under the firmament from the waters which were above the firmament. And it was so. And God called the firmament Heaven. And there was evening and there was morning, a second day.

And God said, 'Let the waters under the heavens be gathered together into one place, and let the dry land appear.' And it was so. God called the dry land Earth, and the waters that were gathered together he called Seas. And God saw that it was good. And God said, 'Let the earth put forth vegetation: plants yielding seed, and fruit trees bearing fruit in which is their seed, each according to its kind, upon the earth.' And it was so. The earth brought forth vegetation, plants yielding seed according to their own kinds, and trees bearing fruit in which is their seed, each according to its kind. And God saw that it was good. And there was evening and there was morning, a third day.

And God said, 'Let there be lights in the firmament of the heavens to separate the day from the night.' . . . and God made the two great lights, the greater light to rule the day, and the lesser light to rule the night . . . And God set them in the firmament of the heavens to give light upon the earth, to rule over the day and over the night, and to separate the light from the darkness.

. . . And there was evening and there was morning, a fourth day.

And God said, 'Let the waters bring forth swarms of living creatures, and let birds fly above the earth across the firmament of the heavens.' So God created the great sea monsters and every living creature that moves, with which the waters swarm, according to their kinds, and every winged bird according to its kind . . . And God blessed them, saying, 'Be fruitful and multiply and fill the waters in the seas, and let birds multiply on the earth.' And there was evening and there was morning, a fifth day.

. . . And God made the beasts of the earth according to their kinds and the cattle according to their kinds, and everything that creeps upon the ground according to its kind. And God saw that it was good.

Then God said, 'Let us make men in our image, after our likeness; and let them have dominion over the fish of the sea, and over the birds of the air, and over the cattle, and over all the earth, and over every creeping thing that creeps upon the earth.' So God created man in his own image, in the image of God he created him; male and female he created them. And God blessed them, and God said to them, 'Be fruitful and multiply, and fill the earth and subdue it; and have dominion over the fish of the sea and over the birds of the air, and over every living thing that moves upon the earth.' . . . And it was so. And God saw everything that he had made, and behold, it was very good. And there was evening and there was morning, a sixth day.

Thus the heavens and the earth were finished, and all the host of them. And on the seventh day God finished his work which he had done, and he rested on the seventh day from all his work which he had done. So God blessed the seventh day and hallowed it, because on it God rested from all his work which he had done in creation.[2]

Here we go. Let us assume the author of that narrative – if there was indeed a single author – was a man: what did he think he was doing when he composed it? What was going through his mind? What was he *thinking?* He did not know, could not have known how or when the world had been created. He had no idea of the unimaginably long stretch of time it took from the Big Bang 13.7 billion years ago till the formation of our planet five billion years ago. Nor could he have had any idea of the pitiless vastness of the universe. He looked up at the sky and saw a *firmament* or dome studded with lights, 'the greater light to rule the day and the lesser light to rule the night and the stars . . . set . . . in the firmament of the heavens to give light upon the earth, to rule over the day and over the night, and to separate the light from the darkness'.

It is worth pausing to imagine what looking up at the dome of the sky felt like for him. It must have been a combination of awe and intimacy. When *we* look up, there is awe certainly, but no longer any intimacy. We know the universe stretches terrifyingly beyond human imagination, perhaps for ever. For the author of Genesis, it was awesome yet contained, almost local. Circumscribed. There was a lid on it, a firmament. From his point of view his description was accurate. Or a good guess at accuracy, though accuracy was scarcely the point. He was an artist, and we know that artists are compelled to re-present reality, to tell it back to itself, to respond to it. Remember Cézanne and the landscape thinking itself through him. In words, the author of Genesis painted what *he* saw. And reading it in an English translation 3,000 years later we can still capture something of the wonder and exhilaration he felt as he gazed up at the night sky.

That's fine for the view, for *what* he saw when he looked up. But how are we to read his account of how it got there and how long it took? Six days! Was he lying? Or guessing or repeating what he had been told? However he arrived at his number, we now know how absurd the idea of a six-day creation is. But the absurdity does not lie in his text. No, the real absurdity lies in how subsequent generations chose to read his words.

I don't think he got the idea from anyone else. I think he made it up, the way writers make up stories all the time. That's what creative artists do. I don't know what he *thought* he was doing as he did it, but I suspect he was being playful. Maybe he made it up as a bedtime story for his children. Or maybe he was improvising at the campfire one night as the villagers gathered round and asked him, their keeper of memories and legends – '*sennachie*' in Gaelic – to give them a story as they sat together under the star-studded dome that curved above their heads. I used to tell my own children tales like that at bedtime. I've made up stories for my local Sunday School, one of them about how the three wise men who came to Bethlehem to find the baby Jesus played the bagpipes as they rode their camels from the mystic East. Grown-up now, one of them will sometimes remind me that it was the bagpipes that clinched the story in their memory. My hunch is that something like that is how it first went down between his hearers and the author of Genesis. It was never meant to be solemnly analysed or interpreted. It was certainly never meant to be 'believed' or taken literally any more than my bagpipe-playing Magi. It was a flourish, an emphasis, the cadence of a poem, a prompter of wonder. Why can't we just read and enjoy it for its own sake and on its own terms like that? Why the clamour of disagreement over its meaning? Why has all the fun gone out of it?

Well, it is because, hundreds of years later, it was hijacked by the leaders of the Christian Church and made to serve another, grimmer purpose. What happened was that these old remembered stories from the waking days of the children of Israel were appropriated by Christian thinkers and used to perpetuate a system they devised for their own theological purposes. The Hebrew scriptures, of which Genesis, meaning beginning, was the prelude or prologue, were an anthology of ancient writings that had slowly accreted over the centuries and achieved their final form hundreds of years before the Church appeared in history. In spite of that long and independent history, the belief established itself among Christians that what they were now being taught to call the Old Testament – 'old' because it had been superseded by a 'new' revelation that relegated it to the status of precursor – had never been what its original editors and writers had thought it was or intended it to be. Unbeknownst to them, God had been using them to craft prophecies of events that would not come to pass for another thousand years, in the birth, teaching, suffering and death of a first-century Nazarene called Jesus who was more than he seemed to be. To those who believed in him he was the '*Messiah*' – Christ in Greek – the One promised to save the world.

Saved from what? From the dire consequences of an impending catastrophe they had discovered in an old Jewish history book. It was an account of humanity's primordial disobedience of God – its original sin – the punishment for which would be eternal damnation unless a rescue attempt were mounted to save humanity from the wrath to come. Let me try to make that clearer, by coming at it the other way around. The Jews had written a book whose tragic import they themselves did not understand. How could they? They had no idea they were merely the pen the divine writer was using. They did not realise that they were not themselves the authors of the story they did not know they were writing. The stories they were writing were in fact a code whose meaning had been revealed to the early Christians, who alone understood the gravity of the situation they revealed and who alone possessed the means for averting the catastrophe they predicted. Because only they were *in the know*.

Time to pause, reflect and ask a few questions. Isn't this what we are all doing all the time, if only in different contexts? Reading contradictory meanings into the events we confront and the different ways we interpret them? And even finding that what we think we've been seeing is not actually what we've been seeing but something else entirely? No, you're not going mad. It *is* that complicated. It is another example of those self-authenticating and self-fortifying psychological states we call *beliefs*. In this case the belief that these ancient Jewish stories, read through the lens of faith, revealed the invisible writing that contained the secret *gnosis* of God's rescue plan for Christians.

Again I have to ask the question: rescue from *what* or from *whom*? The genius of the answer Christian believers give to that question is that it is known only to those who have learned how to read and understand the old stories that contain the secret only they know how to interpret. There is a brilliant circularity about the claim that makes it self-fortifying. There is no way of understanding it from outside; no external validation is available. And none is needed. Because a belief, as we saw in the case of Tony Blair and the Iraq war, carries its own meaning and justification within itself. It is believed because it is believed.

Salvationist Christians believe that the Old Testament is not an accidental collection of texts gradually assembled over millennia that reflects the religious and political history of the people who wrote and compiled it, just like any other library of ancient texts. They believe it is more like the ghost or automatic writing of psychics than the normal compositions of writers personally in charge of what they were doing. The Old Testament had been 'inspired' or 'breathed' by God to be read and understood by a people as yet unborn who would understand its hidden meaning. This is another example of the importance of symbols in religious history. A symbol is an object that stands for, or represents, something else.

It goes without saying, of course, that this is not how Jews, whose ancestors created the 'Old' Testament, understand it. And they have been remarkably generous and forgiving towards those who have appropriated their scriptures for their own purposes. John Barton reminds us that nowhere in the Hebrew texts themselves do they ever claim to have been divinely inspired.[3] In fact, the only place in the whole Bible where a claim to 'inspiration' is found is in the New Testament, the collection of Christian documents produced towards the end of the first century CE that offers a number of different versions of the story of Jesus the Nazarene. It is found in chapter three of the Second Letter to Timothy, where it set the merry-go-round circling by asserting:

All scripture is inspired by God and profitable for teaching, for reproof, for correction, and for training in righteousness . . . [4]

Later Christians would go further and claim that not only had the Old Testament been 'inspired' by God, every word in it had actually been *dictated* by God, so it was inerrant in every detail, *including its account of the creation of the world in six days*. Which brings us back to the story of the six-day creation in the passage from Genesis we are thinking about here.

Apart from the mistake of believing that the Old Testament was a coded message intended to be understood exclusively by them, the other big mistake the early Christians made was in reading its stories literally rather than symbolically, as news reporting rather than as an artistic creation. It was a strange mistake to have made. After all, if the Old Testament was written in a code which only they knew how to interpret, why did they also go on to believe that what it said was historically accurate? They lacked the imagination to picture the Hebrew sennachie practising his craft under the starlit dome and they started, in Roger Scruton's term, *'scientizing'* him: they started reading him not as art but as *gnosis*. Even within their own coded way of understanding the Old Testament, it was a fatal and unnecessary mistake. It was in this way that the hare of a six-day creation started its long surrealist run through history. And it's still running. The tragedy was that because they refused to read Genesis as art – even if it was as an art that pointed exclusively to them – they started to misread it as history, reportage, the notes of a divine journalist who was there on the scene when the world was formed.

It probably did not matter that much till the nineteenth century, when scientists offered compelling evidence that proved the absurdity of belief in a six-day creation or the special place of humans in the lengthy and gradual process. It put the Church on an unnecessary collision course with science and suggested to people that to be a Christian they had to screw themselves up to believe things they knew were not true and deny things they knew were true. In time, the more thoughtful elements of Christianity caught up with the science and acknowledged their mistake, but by then it was too late. People had got used to the idea that Christians were always behind the curve when it came to acknowledging what others had recognised as true ages before. They realised that their resistance to change wasn't due to ordinary conservatism and reluctance to abandon familiar opinions, an attitude we can all understand. It went deeper than that. It was holding on to a mistake *because it had been taught as a divinely mandated truth*. Even when the mistake was admitted by believers in Biblical inerrancy, and they tried to adapt themselves to modern science, they only succeeded in making the absurdity more absurd. This is how some of them respond today.

The Bible says the creation of the world took six days. The Bible is inerrant, so six days it must have been. But we also know from science that creation actually took billions of years, so how do we square the difference? Easy. 'Day' in the Bible was clearly never meant to be understood as 24 hours. It must have meant as long as it took to get the job done – even billions of years. Argument over. And the Bible remains inerrant. Sigh of relief in some quarters. Snort of contempt in others. All because people don't know how to read old stories. Or because they are determined to misread them because they want to go on believing that it was not men but God that wrote them, and God is never wrong.

But even here something in me wants to make room for this naive belief in the historical accuracy of a six-day creation, however believers try to explain it. It is obscurantist, sure. It gives ammunition to people who hate religion and want it laughed out of existence, certainly. And in some places it actively denies children an honest education in science, absolutely. Nevertheless, I want to make space for it, as long as there are no cruel consequences to how the belief is held. There are more dangerous absurdities in life. If some people choose to take this ancient piece of creative writing literally, let them, with the provisos against cruelty noted above. To me it's a waste, that's all. A refusal of imagination. But there are minds that operate that way. Stubbornly literal. Insensitive to the many layers of meaning a text can possess. Let them be. They have their reward.

It was the next example of historicising an old myth that did the real damage. It did more than make Christians look silly. It provoked real cruelties, the effects of which still have a considerable impact today.

V

THE FALL

Here's the next story:

In the day that the Lord God made the earth and the heavens, when no plant of the field was yet in the earth and no herb of the field had yet sprung up – for the Lord God had not caused it to rain upon the earth, and there was no man to till the ground; but a mist went up from the earth, and watered the whole face of the ground – then the Lord God formed man of dust from the ground, and breathed into his nostrils the breath of life; and man became a living being. And the Lord God planted a garden in Eden, in the east; and there he put the man whom he had formed. And out of the ground the Lord God made to grow every tree that is pleasant to the sight and good for food, the tree of life also in the midst of the garden, and the tree of the knowledge of good and evil . . .

The Lord God took the man and put him in the garden of Eden to till it and keep it. And the Lord God commanded the man, saying, 'You may freely eat of every tree of the garden; but of the tree of the knowledge of good and evil you shall not eat, for in the day that you eat of it you shall die.'

Then the Lord God said, 'It is not good that the man should be alone; I will make him a helper fit for him.' . . . So the Lord God caused a deep sleep to fall upon the man, and while he slept took one of his ribs and closed up its place with flesh; and the rib which the Lord God had taken from the man he made into a woman and brought her to the man. Then the man said,

'This at last is bone of my bones
and flesh of my flesh;
she shall be called Woman,
because she was taken out of Man.'

Therefore a man leaves his father and his mother and cleaves to his wife, and they become one flesh. And the man and his wife were both naked, and were not ashamed.

Now the serpent was more subtle than any other wild creature that the Lord God had made. He said to the woman, 'Did God say, "You shall not eat of any tree in the garden"?' And the woman said to the serpent, 'We may eat of the fruit of the trees in the garden; but God said, "You shall not eat of the fruit of the tree which is in the midst of the garden, neither shall you touch it, lest you die."' But the serpent said to the woman, 'You will die. For God knows that when you eat of it your eyes will be opened, and you will be like God, knowing good and evil.' So when the woman saw that the tree was good for food, and that it was a delight to the eyes, and that the tree was to be desired to make one wise, she took of its fruit and ate; and she also gave some to her husband, who was with her, and he ate. Then the eyes of both were opened, and they knew that they were naked; and they sewed fig leaves together and made themselves aprons.

And they heard the sound of the Lord God walking in the garden in the cool of the day, and the man and his wife hid themselves from the presence of the Lord God among the trees of the garden. But the Lord God called to the man, and said to him, 'Where are you?' And he said, 'I heard the sound of thee in the garden, and I was afraid, because I was naked; and I hid myself.' He said, 'Who told you that you were naked? Have you eaten of the tree of which I commanded you not to eat?' The man said, 'The woman whom thou gavest to be with me, she gave me fruit of the tree, and I ate.' Then the Lord God said to the woman, 'What is this that you have done?' The woman said, 'The serpent beguiled me, and I ate.' The Lord God said to the serpent,

'Because you have done this, cursed are you above
    all cattle,
and above all wild animals;
upon your belly you shall go,
and dust you shall eat
all the days of your life.
I will put enmity between you and the woman,
and between your seed and her seed;

he shall bruise your head,
and you shall bruise his heel.'

To the woman he said,

'I will greatly multiply your pain in childbearing;
in pain you shall bring forth children,
yet your desire shall be for your husband,
and he shall rule over you.'

And to Adam he said,

'Because you have listened to the voice of your wife,
and have eaten of the tree
of which I commanded you,
"You shall not eat of it,"
cursed is the ground because of you;
in toil you shall eat of it all the days of your life;
thorns and thistles it shall bring forth for you;
and you shall eat the plants of the field.
In the sweat of your face
you shall eat bread
till you return to the ground,
for out of it you were taken;
you are dust,
and to dust you shall return.'

The man called his wife's name Eve, because she was the
mother of all living. And the Lord God made for Adam
and for his wife garments of skins, and clothed them.

Then the Lord God said, 'Behold, the man has

become like one of us, knowing good and evil; and now, lest he put forth his hand and take also of the tree of life, and eat, and live for ever' – therefore the Lord God sent him forth from the garden of Eden, to till the ground from which he was taken. He drove out the man; and at the east of the garden of Eden he placed the cherubim, and a flaming sword which turned every way, to guard the way to the tree of life.[1]

Before exploring the meaning of this story, I want to begin with a question. What did the author or the authors of this story think they were doing when they composed it? We know now it did not happen the way they described it. We know that our emergence in the world was not a swift and single event, the immediate result of a divine fiat one afternoon at the beginning of creation. Of course, the author did not know then what we know now. But nor could he have known even then *what did not happen*. What did not happen cannot be *known*, though it may be *believed*. So what's going on here, what is the author up to? Is he lying? Too simple. Mendacity and ignorance are not the same thing. Is he just passing on a story he inherited? Probably, but that does not help us figure out the meaning of the story either, and how we might use or interpret it. *And this is a story that matters.* It's a story that has had, and continues to have, a devastating effect in history. Unlike the narrative of a six-day creation, misreading the story of Adam and Eve in the Garden of Eden has been more than silly or eccentric, it has been actively dangerous. It has hurt women. It continues to hurt them. And it shows how bad stories can kill people. Or to put it another way, it shows how good stories read badly, read the wrong way, can be poisonous. This one has been a real killer in history. We talk nowadays about 'toxic masculinity', and for good reason. Men have always made the world an unsafe place for women. There are many reasons for that, but one of them can be found in how an influential generation of Christian leaders infused their own obsession with sex and consequent hatred of women into an old myth, and sent it into history to spread its stain.

That's why there's a lot to pick through here, but before taking a look at the story itself, I want to begin with a distinction made by many scholars when they approach a text like this. They call it a 'myth', and the first thing they want us to understand is that a myth is not a lie or a delusion, though that has become one of its modern uses. 'That's just a myth,' we say, when challenging the veracity of an event, or some claim to special status by a particular group. Thus, we might talk about the myth of American exceptionalism or the myth of the white man's burden from the days of the British Empire, examples of the delusions nations so easily fall into.

For scholars of religion, a myth is not an untruth, a falsehood. It is a story, a fiction, through which a perennial truth is communicated. Karen Armstrong defines a myth as, 'A timeless truth that happens all the time'. It's a made-up story intended to cast light on the human condition. But I have a question about that definition. Did their original writers know they were fashioning *myths*, in our understanding of the term, when they made up their stories? I wonder. I wonder if this is not another instance of us reading our own preferences into the minds of these old authors, of finding what we want to find in them and seeing what we want to see. A bit of me thinks these old writers knew exactly what they were doing when they told their tales, but not in the sense that they thought to themselves, 'I am now going to craft a story that carries a hidden meaning which I want my readers to figure out for themselves.' I suspect it was less calculated than that, less thought-through, more spontaneous. Maybe even a kind of possession or trance, as if the story had taken the writers over and used them as its instrument.

Some artists claim to have been used in this way when producing their best work. Musicians 'hear' a tune in their heads and rush to get it down before it fades away. Some writers are invaded by a phrase and follow it like a trail of breadcrumbs to wherever it takes them. I have spoken to distinguished painters who told me that some of their work just poured out of them onto the canvas in a manic rush they found it hard to keep up with. I suspect that's how the great religious visions and revelations came to the prophets and seers in the caves or on the mountain tops to which they had retreated in search of meaning. High on the ecstasy of longing and self-abnegation, visions came to them, and art made itself through them. Maybe this is how it went with the Genesis writers, and later generations read universal meanings into their work. It is also possible that these writers were trying to answer fundamental questions about the human condition. Why are women weaker than men? Why is childbirth so painful and dangerous? And a story was made up to explain or account for the situation. That's what humans seem always to have done wherever they found themselves. They told themselves stories to explain the mysteries of their own existence. But they also told them because humans loved listening to them. That's why it is not always easy to figure out exactly what they thought they were doing when they were doing it. In this book I am confining myself to influential stories from the Hebrew scriptures and the use the Christian Church later made of them, but it will be interesting to compare them with another tradition of explanatory myth-making, one with similarities as well as differences: Greek mythology. So let's turn to one of their myths to see if it can be read as a timeless truth that happens all the time.

The Greeks were polytheists. There was a top god called Zeus, god of the sky, who had two partners, Poseidon, god of the sea, and Hades, god of the underworld, the place humans went to when they died. In one of their stories, Hades is desperate for a wife with whom to share his gloomy estate. He abducts Persephone, daughter of Demeter, goddess of fruit, crops and vegetation, and brings her underground to live with him. But Demeter is so devastated by the loss of her daughter that she goes into deep mourning and neglects her duties. As a result, crops fail, fruit vanishes from the trees and humanity is threatened with famine and death. To save the situation, Zeus intervenes and works out a deal that gives each side in the dispute half of what they want. Persephone is sentenced to spend half the year on earth and half the year in the underworld with her boring husband. When summer is over and she descends to Hades to do her time there, her mother Demeter again mourns her absence. Winter strikes the earth and all growing things die. Leaves fall. Trees become bare, fields barren. But in the spring when Persephone ascends to the earth again, her mother rejoices at her return and everything comes back to life.

This is a good example of how a myth crafted to account for the workings of nature can also be used to express the ups and downs of a human life. Human existence has its rhythms of loss and recovery, failure and success, death and rebirth. It's a story that can be understood in different ways. Did the Greeks take it literally? Some of them, probably. Others would have read it in a different way. It was a *story*. And stories can be interpreted in different ways. They can carry many meanings. But what the original authors of the Greek and Hebrew myths we've been looking at thought they were doing is impossible for us to tell. Whether they were consciously crafting myths that were *intended* to carry hidden meanings we cannot now say for sure, but that does not stop us reading them that way today.

But in the Hebrew tradition we do have stories that were precisely calculated to carry a hidden message, a form of utterance popular with the prophets of ancient Israel. Another word for a story intended to carry a hidden meaning is 'parable', from the Greek meaning to cast over or lasso. Think of a parabola and you'll get the idea. A parable was a story that was designed to rope the attention of the hearers and pull them towards a moment of recognition and deeper understanding. A clear example is the story of an encounter between King David and the prophet Nathan, recounted in the Second Book of Samuel. David had seduced a woman called Bathsheba. To cover up his adultery and keep her for himself, he had her husband killed. Nathan the prophet goes to him and tells him the story of a rich landowner who possessed many herds of sheep and cattle. One of his tenants was a poor man whose sole possession was a tiny ewe lamb he loved like a daughter. When a friend arrived unexpectedly for dinner with the rich man, rather than slaughtering one of his own beasts to feed him, he took the poor man's lamb and cooked it for his guest. When King David heard the story, he leapt to his feet angrily and demanded to know the name of the monster who had committed such a crime so that he could be brought to justice. '*You* are the man,' replied Nathan.[2] It worked. David owned his guilt and tried to make what amends he could.

There was a long tradition of devices like that in the history of Israel. Stories that carried meanings deeper than the literal or surface narrative. Parables and myths. Stories that carried other stories, other meanings within them. But can we cram everything we find in Genesis into that pot? For instance, would the story of a six-day creation we discussed in the last chapter make more sense if we read it as a myth or parable? I don't see how, except for one possible reading. Maybe we could understand 'six days' as code for God's sustaining activity, God's constant upholding of the creation through time. A bit of a stretch, maybe, but not an impossible one. But why didn't the writer just say 'in the beginning God created the heavens and the earth and through his goodness he will sustain it till the end of time', and leave it at that? Why the six-day timetable, except as an imaginative little flourish of the sort creative writers can never resist? That's my hunch, anyway. That's why I left him at the campfire with his friends as they looked up at the star-studded canopy above them while he let his story unfold.

Serious scholars don't like that kind of whimsical uncertainty. They like things neatly explained and packaged. Or they like the explanations they themselves have come up with. I think a lot of that is going on in how they wield the myth idea. They want these old stories to make some kind of consistent sense, so they impose their own preferred meanings upon them – and the myth idea is a great way to do it. I just don't think that's what most of these old writers thought they were doing, however. I suspect some of them didn't know *what* they were doing. The stories just came through them or out of them, that's all. Like the man in Molière's play *Le Bourgeois Gentilhomme*, who hadn't realised he'd been speaking prose all his life, these old storytellers didn't know they were creating myths as they sat by the fire spinning their tales.

Except I think the author of the Adam and Eve story may have known what he was doing when he told it. He was describing an event, supposedly in past time, that carried a meaning for all time. It must have happened like this back then, he thought, because he saw it happening right now before his eyes. That's how humans were and always had been. Flawed, discontented souls who were never at peace anywhere, even in Eden, that place round the bend of the river where the cottonwoods grew.

If there's a myth anywhere in the Hebrew scriptures, this has to be it. But was its author self-consciously aware that he was spinning a parable, a story with a hidden meaning in it, on that night by the fire? I suspect he probably was. I think he meant it to be understood as something that happened at all times and in all places, including the village he and his listeners lived in. (Yes, and in the street where you live, maybe even in the house with your name on the door.) The story of Adam and Eve is a parable of the discontent that has broken relationships and destroyed harmony in every human community that has ever existed. Read intelligently, its meaning is never out of date. That's how creative fictions work. They are always about *us*, here and now, in this place and at this time, as well as about former times in other places. They are, in Karen Armstrong's phrase, examples of 'A timeless truth that happens all the time'.

Tragically, a failure or refusal to understand how myths actually work crept into Christianity. Its preachers claimed that these ancient writings were not *art*, the imaginative expression of enduring truths about the human condition. They were reports of events that happened precisely as they were described, right down to a talking snake and a god who walked in a garden in the cool of the early evening. The story of Adam and Eve in the Garden of Eden was converted from an enduringly useful fiction into a dangerous assertion of historical fact. In their account, it wasn't the fact that it went on happening now that mattered. It was that it had definitely happened *then* exactly as described that counted. They took their eyes off its meaning for today and focused them entirely on what was alleged to have happened back then. Nietzsche described how the process started and the loss that resulted.

. . . it is the lot of all myths to creep gradually into the confines of a supposedly historical reality, and to be treated by some later age as unique fact with claims to historical truth . . . this is how religions tend to die: the mythic premises of a religion are systematized, beneath the stern and intelligent eyes of an orthodox dogmatism, into a fixed sum of historical events; one begins nervously defending the veracity of myths, at the same time resisting their continuing life and growth. The feeling for myth dies and is replaced by religious claims to foundation in history.[3]

Nietzsche's final sentence in that quotation, 'The feeling for myth dies and is replaced by religious claims to foundation in history,' is a good place to start thinking about what happened to the myth of Adam and Eve in the Garden of Eden in Christianity's use of the story.

When I quoted John Barton's description of Christianity as a religion of salvation, I asked the question, 'salvation from what?' and said the answer lay in how the early Christians had read a historic catastrophe into the Hebrew scriptures. It was in the Garden of Eden that they identified the event from whose consequences they sought rescue. They read it not as a story that carried a universal human meaning but, in Nietzsche's words, as a 'historical reality'. They read it as an account of a real event that had happened in real time in a real place to a real couple, the clincher being that its consequences were grim not only for them but for the whole human race. It was the beginning of humanity's 'original sin', a fall from a state of innocence and grace into a state of guilt that would infect every human being born in the world till the end of time, when the grand eschatological climax would ensue and the secrets of all hearts would be revealed. In the long and menacing in-between-time while we waited for the promised end, humans had been given the opportunity to be purged of the sin they were guilty of *by virtue of having been born*. According to this telling of the story, birth itself was the source of their woe and the guarantee of their damnation, unless they were rescued by the application of the Christian 'gnosis', the secret formula that alone had the power to dissolve the deadly traces of their inherited guilt. There are many weird elements in this Christian phantasmagoria, but there are several worth looking at here.

The first is found in commentaries on this story in letters from the first Christian writer. He is known to history as Saint Paul the Apostle, a first-century Jewish convert to Christianity, whose epistles to his converts are the earliest writing in the collection of material known as the New Testament. Paul's letters were written sometime between 54 and 58 CE, and they contain several significant mentions of the Adam and Eve story, which he seems to have understood as a historical event that had consequences for the whole human race. This is a bit of a surprise, because Paul had a versatile and interesting mind that rarely stuck to conventional interpretations, but maybe all it shows here is that the Adam and Eve story was by this time understood as a historical event in Christian circles. And perhaps among Jews as well, although Jews have always been proverbially dissonant and varied in how they interpreted their own scriptures. The saying 'Two Jews, three opinions' was as true then as it is now.

At the time he was writing his letters, Paul's big problem was death. Not in the usual way, not because it ends our lives and prompts our sorrow, but because it had become a *theological* problem for Christians at the time. They had been told that they would not die, because Jesus had conquered death for his disciples, and he would be back soon to take them straight into God's coming kingdom. At the end of this book I'll explore where this kind of thinking came from, but for the moment it is enough to say that Paul and the first Christians believed Jesus was God's special agent who had been sent to announce the End Times that would close history and inaugurate God's reign of justice and peace. And they expected this programme of events to be tied up during their own lifetimes. The problem was that some of them had started dying, and the great return had still not occurred. Did this mean that these dead Christians would miss out on entrance into the promised dispensation? That's the problem Paul addresses in the first of his letters to the Corinthians, the earliest text in the New Testament, probably written around 55 CE, twenty years after the death of Jesus – when there was still no sign of his return. Paul addresses the difficulty in the famous fifteenth chapter of this epistle, read at Christian funerals the world over, its two great defiant protests still able to stir the blood of the most sceptical listener: 'O death, where is thy victory? O death, where is thy sting?'

A few verses before these plangent rhetorical questions, Paul mentions Adam in what seems to be a throwaway remark, but is actually one with a deep critical background.

For as by a man came death, by a man has come also the resurrection of the dead.

For as in Adam all die, so also in Christ shall all be made alive.[4]

The meaning behind that sudden claim is unpacked in the Epistle to the Romans, a letter probably written a couple of years later than the First Letter of Paul to the Corinthians, and one with a more developed theology. Here are verses from the relevant passage.

Therefore as sin came into the world through one man and death through sin, and so death spread to all men because all men sinned . . . death reigned . . . even over those whose sins were not like the transgression of Adam, who was a type of the one who was to come . . . If, because of one man's trespass, death reigned through that one man, much more will those who receive the abundance of grace and the free gift of righteousness reign in life through the one man Jesus Christ.[5]

All I want to register from that dense and convoluted passage is Paul's claim that it was because of Adam's disobedience that death entered the world. The implication being that Adam and Eve would have lived deathless lives had they not been tempted by the serpent to eat of the fruit of the forbidden tree. But they did eat of it, so they died, death being the punishment for their sin. Then comes the kicker: *and so death spread to all men because all men sinned.* A glorious non-sequitur, if I've ever seen one. Is Paul saying *we* die, because we also sin? Or we die, because *Adam* sinned? That's certainly what he seems to be saying . . . *because of one man's trespass, death reigned through that one man*. Which suggests that all of us have, somehow, inherited Adam's guilt and responsibility, which is why we die.

I know this is dizzying stuff. And I know that if you take a hand in this theological card game it can keep you fascinated for a lifetime. The point to note is that, whatever sense you make of what Paul is saying, he was clearly working from a historicised understanding of the Adam and Eve story. It had happened as described. Not only did it happen as described, it had consequences that have bled into the lives of all humans born since the original offence – the big one being that that's why we all die. The assumption being that if Adam had not sinned, he would not have died, and nor would we.

I am not interested in trying to make sense of Paul's weird logic here, because I want to press on to a more significant development in the interpretation of this passage by Christian thinkers a few hundred years later. For Paul the big story was death. It had entered the world because of Adam's sin. His problem was not its origin in Adam, which he took for granted. His problem was that for Christians it wasn't supposed to go on happening, because Christ was coming back for them. But he hadn't turned up. Still hasn't. The Church found a way of living with the unexplained delay, because human belief systems are good at absorbing contradictions into their thinking. The appropriate conditions have not yet aligned. Or there has been a misunderstanding. I continue to find something moving in this human capacity for hope. Especially in the face of death. Which is why I am always touched when I read Paul's great withstanding of death in his First Letter to the Corinthians.

> Lo! I tell you a mystery. We shall not all sleep, but we shall all be changed, in a moment, in the twinkling of an eye, at the last trumpet. For the trumpet will sound, and the dead shall be raised imperishable, and we shall be changed.[6]

Who can blame him for raising his fist against death, the great destroyer of our joy and plunderer of our hopes? Hatred of death I can understand. Which is why I admire Paul for standing astride the grave and hurling his defiance into the wind.

I feel differently about those who came after him and hurtled their imprecations not against death, but against sex. Their obsession with sex started the real Christian phantasmagoria. Paul told us that had there been no Fall, no disobedience, there would have been no death. And he hated death. What these later thinkers told us was that had there been no Fall, there would have been no sex. Or no sex as we experience it. Sex without concupiscence. Sex without desire. Without pleasure. Sex, in fact, without sex. Here are the bits of the Genesis story they fastened on to make their point:

> the Lord God called to the man, and said to him, 'Where are you?' And he said, 'I heard the sound of thee in the garden, *and I was afraid, because I was naked;* and I hid myself.' He said, 'Who told you that you were naked?

Have you eaten of the tree of which I commanded you not to eat?' The man said, 'The woman whom thou gavest to be with me, she gave me fruit of the tree, and I ate.' Then the Lord God said to the woman, 'What is this that you have done?' The woman said, 'The serpent beguiled me, and I ate.'

There you have it. 'Who told you that you were naked?' The beginning of sex is the catastrophe, the real Fall from asexual innocence to incessant desire. Because of it, God says to the woman, 'I will greatly multiply your pains in childbearing; in pain you shall bring forth children, yet your desire shall be for your husband, and *he shall rule over you*.' This way of reading the story is made quite explicit in the First Letter to Timothy in the New Testament, a document attributed to Saint Paul but almost certainly not written by him, though it reflected his views.

Let a woman learn in silence with all submissiveness. I permit no woman to teach or have authority over men; she is to keep silent. For Adam was formed first, then Eve; and Adam was not deceived, but the woman was deceived and became a transgressor. Yet woman will be saved through bearing children, if she continues in faith and love and holiness, with modesty.[7]

I could see the original telling of this story working like this, as our Hebrew sennachie spun his yarn that night by the fire and under the stars. Maybe he was asked why childbirth was so hard and why women were controlled and dominated by men and why farming was such backbreaking work. Why was life so tough? Well, he began, once upon a time, our ancestors the first man and the first woman didn't have to work at all because they lived in a garden where all was provided. But one day . . .

It's hardly a perfect explanation, but I can see it working as a story with a bit of a moral to it, a hidden meaning. Peasant societies are never without their discontents, their rivalries and errant desires. There would be truths they could all connect with in this telling. There might even have been furtive, knowing glances passing between them, as they listened to the story. It's what later Christians made of it that did the real damage. They read it not as a time-less truth that happens all the time, but as an actual event specific to a particular moment in history, and their misreading of the story was to have a devastating effect on women down the years. Misreading the story not only gave divine authority to the silencing and subordinating of women to men – as that passage from the First Letter to Timothy makes clear – it went on to impart inherited guilt to the whole human race. Because Adam was deceived by Eve and sinned, we all inherit the blame and the consequences.

How do you get from Adam and Eve to you and me in that statement? To heighten the absurdity, let me put it another way. Say, years before I was born, my parents had a drug-running cartel, for which they were tried, found guilty and did time. Years later I am born. I grow up. One day there's a knock at the door. Two policemen arrest me and take me to court where I am found guilty of the crimes my parents committed thirty years before. 'How can I be guilty of crimes that happened before I was even thought of?' I ask. 'Haven't you heard?' they reply. 'It has been decreed that henceforth all children inherit the guilt for any crimes committed by their parents, even before they were born. It is called "original crime". And since we are all related, one way or another, to everyone who ever was, we are all guilty of that original offence. We were born therefore we are guilty.'

Or say your parents suffered from an incurable, transmissible disease they had brought on themselves because of their disordered lives. In the circumstances, they should never have had children, but they did. You were born and you've inherited their disease, whether you like it or not. And here's the consequence: *if you have sex, you'll pass it on as well.* At last we've got to the issue that preoccupied these Christian thinkers.

Though they often deny it, faith communities are affected by changes in the surrounding culture. They are permeable to new ways of thinking, both negatively and positively. Somewhere between the writing of the New Testament and the fifth century a strange anxiety entered Christianity's attitude towards human sexuality. It may have leached in from the confusion and anxiety that accompanied the gradual decline and fall of the Roman Empire. History is studded with these eras of hectic disintegration, the early twentieth century being a good example. The prevailing sense that something is ending and something worse is dawning spawns all sorts of reactions, from world-denying asceticism to fevered excess. In religious communities these ages of anxiety usually prompt an in-turning against the world as the deformed creation of a fallen spirit. However we account for it, it was through this dark lens in a turbulent period that the story of Adam and Eve and the serpent in the Garden of Eden was read by some influential Christian theologians in the fifth century CE.

It was Eve who had accepted the forbidden fruit offered by the serpent. It was Eve who lured innocent Adam into sex, thereby transmitting guilt to him and through him to the whole human race. This way of reading the ancient myth established the idea that woman was the source of man's misery, and his desire for her was a constant danger to his soul. This is how the syllogism was parsed: *everyone born is born guilty of original sin. Sex is the mechanism through which they were conceived. Therefore, sex is the cause of their guilt.*

One of the main proponents of this way of reading the myth was Augustine, Bishop of Hippo in North Africa in the fifth century, one of the geniuses of early Christianity and a man troubled by his own demons of longing and regret. Though many Christians already believed that the 'first sin' of Adam had been inherited by all Adam's descendants – the whole human race – it was Augustine who told them precisely where they should look in their own bodies for clinging evidence of this first sin. The great Augustinian scholar Peter Brown noted that

> . . . with the fatal ease of a man who believes that he can explain a complex phenomenon, simply by reducing it to its historical origins, Augustine will remind his congregation of the exact circumstances of the Fall of Adam and Eve. When they had disobeyed God by eating the forbidden fruit, they had been 'ashamed': they had covered their genitals with fig leaves. That was enough

for Augustine: 'Ecce unde'. 'That's the place! That's the place from which the first sin is passed on.'[8]

Augustine believed that had Adam and Eve never eaten of the tree of the knowledge of good and evil, they would have propagated children 'without shame at the uncontrollable stirring of their genitals'. Procreation would have been without pleasure or desire. In fact, without sex:

> This urge, had it existed in Paradise . . . would . . . have never run beyond the bidding of the will . . . It would never have forced itself upon the mind with thoughts of inappropriate and impermissible delights. It would not have had to be held upon the leash by married moderation, or fought to a draw by ascetic labour. Rather, when once called for, it would have followed the will of the person with all the ease of a single-hearted act of obedience.[9]

Why did sex become such an obsession with men like Augustine and others of his generation? There are myths in other cultures that try to account for the force and disturbing power of sexual attraction, but they did not trap us in this kind of hatred of our own desires. In classical Greek thought, sexuality was understood to be potentially excessive by nature, so the moral question was always how to control it, how to regulate its economy in an appropriate way. This was not achieved by legislation that permitted or forbade certain acts, but by the achievement of an art of living that involved the individual in a battle to achieve dominion of the self over the self. Self-overcoming was freely chosen for the sake of the self, just like any other discipline. It was never characterised by the anguish we find in the Christian struggle with sexuality, which loads it with so much danger that it creates an ethic of anxiety and suspicion.

It might be useful to compare it to the need to eat, another appetite that can go badly wrong. Eating can demonstrate a number of human pathologies. Some people eat themselves into a state of morbid excess; some people suffer from complex eating disorders and starve themselves to death; others use eating as an emotional substitute or compensation for losses in their lives. Most of us would accept the need for a sensible and sustainable ethic of eating that balanced the importance of eating for health and survival with the dangers of eating the wrong thing, eating to excess or not eating at all. Or having a diet that did not damage the ecosystem on which we all depend for survival. We would not see eating as problematic in itself, though we would recognise that the human genius for pathologising nature will apply here as well.

The distinctive thing about the Christian ethic of sexuality is that it was seen by some of its most significant thinkers as intrinsically sinful, as the vehicle that transmitted the virus of original sin through history. In their exegesis of Genesis, these thinkers rendered *any* expression of human sexuality as problematic. It was not a question of more or less, appropriate or inappropriate sex. It was between a No and a Yes to sex, in which the Yes, even when licensed by marriage, was seen as the lesser of two evils, a concession to human weakness. This, in fact, is how it was described in the wedding service in the Book of Common Prayer:

> Marriage was ordained for a remedy against sin, and to avoid fornication; that such persons as have not the gift of continency might marry, and keep themselves undefiled members of Christ's body.

Even this concession was grudgingly conceded in some quarters. Saint Jerome, 345–420 CE, observed that the only good thing that could be said about marriage was that it bred virgins. A weird eschatology of virginity began to emerge in the Church. If only everyone could be persuaded to abstain from sex and remain virgin, maybe the Fall would be undone, history would end and Eden would be restored.

There have been many consequences of this Christian historicising of an obvious myth, but one of the grimmest was that women, especially post-menopausal women, were held to be peculiarly liable to the sin of witchcraft, a secret power to harm or kill their neighbours through an alliance with supernatural diabolic agencies. Witches were imagined as flying through the air at night to their secret covens, where they concocted their plans to harm others and interfere with the benign forces of nature to achieve their maleficent ends. Augustine, among other early Christian thinkers, believed in their existence. But for reasons that are not entirely clear, the Church in the Middle Ages became obsessed with the idea. Across a period of 250 years, it is estimated that 50,000 witches were executed in Europe, 500 of them in England, 1,500 in Scotland. The last woman executed for witchcraft in England was in 1684, in Scotland in 1727.

The theory behind the craze was made brutally explicit in the *Malleus Maleficarum*, or *Hammer of the Witches*, a handbook for witch-finders and inquisitors written by two Dominican friars in 1486. It began by quoting a text from the book of Sirach in the Apocrypha on the inherent wickedness of women, clearly based on a literal reading of the story of the Fall. 'Sin began with a woman, and because of her we all die.'[10] Then, to support their claim that woman is the source of sin, they quote a misogynistic rant of Saint John Chrysostom, Patriarch of Constantinople, at the very end of the fourth century:

> What else is woman but a foe to friendship, an inescapable punishment, a necessary evil, a natural temptation, a desirable calamity, a domestic danger, a delectable detriment, an evil of nature painted with fair colours!

It is obvious that they are really talking about their guilty longing for sex here, that irresistible 'calamity' for which they blame woman. The woman gave me and I did eat. The woman lured me and I did . . . place the verb of your choice in the space provided. Here they go with the blame game:

> If the world would be rid of women, to say nothing of witchcraft, it would remain proof against innumerable dangers . . . I have found a woman more bitter than death . . . and as the sin of Eve would not have

brought death to our souls and body unless the sin had afterward been passed to Adam, to which he was tempted by Eve, not by the devil, therefore is she more bitter than death. More bitter than death, again, because that is natural and destroys the body, but the sin which arose from woman destroys the soul by depriving it of grace, and delivers the body up to the punishment for sin. More bitter than death, again, because bodily death is an open and terrible enemy, but woman is a secret and wheedling enemy. All witchcraft comes from carnal lust, which in woman is insatiable.[11]

Sex was no longer a natural appetite that could go wrong if not handled with care; it was now understood as a temptation that should *never* be yielded to. Man's tragedy, his original sin, was that he could not help desiring women, but if he gave in to his desire, he fell into a sin that endangered his salvation and would certainly show him to be a moral weakling. It is not hard to see how such a prohibition would turn men into haters of women. Saint John Chrysostom captured the male dilemma perfectly. Woman was not looked upon as a potential friend or lover or companion, let alone an equal, but as, 'A natural temptation, a desirable calamity, a delectable detriment'.

This was the beginning of the exaltation of celibacy that dominated the thinking of the Church for centuries. Strong and spiritual men did not have sex; they spurned the delectable lures of woman for a higher purpose. They repressed their sexuality and preserved their purity. But if a man was not up to this level of heroism and self-denial, if he did not possess what the Church called 'the

gift of continency', then he might marry; it was better
to marry than to burn. But it was seen as a concession
for the weak. From that tragic distortion much sorrow
and abuse and hatred poured and continues to surge
through enquiry after enquiry in our own day. There are
few straight men who won't have occasion to include
themselves in this ancient roll-call of blame. That is why
it has become one of the great purposes of our time to
purge ourselves of that history and its consequences.
And not only in Christianity. We are beginning to come
to terms with the difficulty of achieving a just balance
in our sexual relations, and part of that adjustment has
to be acknowledgement by men of the misery their lust
to control and enjoy women on their own terms has
caused.

And all this over *something that never happened, except in the
imaginations of a writer, except in the pages of a fiction.* No
serpent. No tree of the knowledge of good and evil. No
innocently naked man and woman. Just a story. A myth
that needs interpreting but should never be read literally.
But that's precisely how these Christian thinkers read it,
and it cast a web of suspicion over human sexuality that
loaded it with complexity and sullied it with unnecessary
guilt. William Blake caught the tragedy of it all in three
simple verses:

I went to the Garden of Love,
And saw what I never had seen:
A chapel was built in the midst
Where I used to play on the green.

And the gates of this chapel were shut,
And 'Thou shalt not' writ over the door;
So I turned to the Garden of Love
That so many sweet flowers bore,

And I saw it was filled with graves,
And tomb-stones where flowers should be,
And priests in black gowns, were walking their
    rounds,
And binding with briars my joys and desires.[12]

Astonishing what can come from not knowing how to read an old story. Or from reading an old story the wrong way. No wonder the millennial generations in Europe and the United States have such contempt for the priests in black gowns who would bind with briars their joys and desires. Especially since so many of them have been spectacularly unsuccessful at binding their own.

Another tragedy in this is that because priests in black gowns so cruelly misread and misinterpreted these old stories from the Bible, they have deprived future generations of the wisdom and guidance that can also be found in them when read and interpreted in other ways. It brings us back again to the ruthlessness of the idea of sanctioned truths, exclusive ways of understanding the mystery of existence, as ordained by the officers of religious institutions. Fortunately, priests have never had it all their own way in the history of religion. There have always been men and women who put more trust in the validity of their own intuitions and spiritual experiences than in the sanctioned truths of dogmatic religion. We call them mystics.

PART III

STORIES THE MYSTICS TELL

VI

APOLLO AND DIONYSUS

O n the afternoon of 6 June 1968, I visited the Haight-Ashbury district of San Francisco to watch the hippies and get a feel for what was being described as America's countercultural revolution. It was an ominous day for the visit, the day Robert Kennedy died. He'd been shot the night before in Los Angeles after winning the Democratic presidential primary, only weeks after Martin Luther King had been assassinated and rioting had erupted in many American cities. Middle America was in despair over what its revolting children were up to, though it seemed to have fewer qualms about pouring fire onto the people of Vietnam.

What I witnessed that day was a Dionysian carnival of opposition both to the American state and to the state of America. The carnival was obviously beginning to spin out of control, yet it was also strangely moving. All those lost children getting high on protest and escape, the polar opposite of their tense Apollonian parents who were baffled by what was happening to their country. Like many other human archetypes, these labels, and the disjunctions they point to, come from Greek mythology. Apollo and Dionysus were sons of the top god, Zeus. Apollo, god of the sun, represented order and rationality. Dionysus, god of wine and dance, represented chaos and irrationality. Nietzsche had used them as human archetypes in his first book, *The Birth of Tragedy*. This is how Sue Prideaux describes the tension he was defining:

> . . . just as procreation depends on the duality of the sexes, so the continuing development of art and culture down the ages depends on the duality of the Apollonian and the Dionysian. Like the two sexes, they are engaged in a continual struggle interrupted only by temporary periods of reconciliation . . . the qualities of Apollo can be summed up more or less as the apparent, the describable . . . the representative . . .
>
> Dionysus . . . represented an enchanted world . . . transcending existential boundaries . . . Music and tragedy are both capable of erasing the individual spirit and awakening impulses which in their heightened forms cause the subjective to dwindle into complete self-oblivion, while the spirit is mystically transported to a transcendent state of bliss or horror.[1]

Self-oblivion was certainly one of the aims of the hippies in Haight-Ashbury. A year before me, Joan Didion had been there with her notebook, where she had met a five-year-old child on acid.

> The five-year-old's name is Susan, and she tells me she is in High Kindergarten. She lives with her mother and some other people, just got over the measles, wants a bicycle for Christmas, and particularly likes Coca-Cola

ice cream . . . For a year her mother has given her acid and peyote. Susan describes it as getting stoned.[2]

But the counterculture was about more than getting laid and getting stoned. It was also a pursuit of transcendence, even if it would turn into a transcendence of horror, another phantasmagoria. Didion, one of the first to figure out what was going on, quotes a psychiatrist:

> Anybody who thinks this is all about drugs has his head in a bag. It's a social movement, quintessentially romantic, the kind that recurs in times of real social crisis. The themes are always the same. A return to innocence. The invocation of an earlier authority and control. The mysteries of the blood. An itch for the transcendental, for purification. Right there you've got the ways that romanticism historically ends up in trouble, lends itself to authoritarianism. When the direction appears. How long do you think it'll take for that to happen?[3]

It actually didn't take much longer for the romanticism to end in the kind of tragedy the psychiatrist had predicted. Just over a year after my visit, on 9 August 1969, at 10500 Cielo Drive in Los Angeles, a gang of counter-cultural misfits in thrall to a hypnotic narcissist called Charles Manson hacked five people to death, including a heavily pregnant film star called Sharon Tate. Though its protests would continue till the Vietnam War came to its inglorious end in 1975, the romantic innocence of the counterculture was effectively over. Apollo and Dionysus had again fought themselves to a draw.

But this hadn't been the United States's first counter-cultural rebellion or face-off between Apollo and Dionysus. They'd had one forty years earlier, though its Dionysian protesters hadn't gathered on the streets of Haight-Ashbury to act out their contempt. They had gone into exile in Paris, the so-called lost generation after the First World War, determined to reject the values that had wrecked the world they were inheriting.

> They gave us this thing, knocked to pieces, leaky, red-hot, threatening to blow up; and then they are surprised that we don't accept it with the same attitude of pretty, decorous enthusiasm with which they received it . . .[4]

These romantic exiles abroad embraced the sins Middle America loathed to the depths of its Northern Protestant soul, the sins of the south, the sins of the wrong sort of immigrant:

> . . . adultery, profanity, homosexuality, divorce, alcohol, extravagance, perversity, drugs, individuality, liberty and libertinism.[5]

In time, the lost generation's romantic rebellion also came to an end, and they made their way home to the USA, another revolution over, another score-draw between Apollo and Dionysus. Some fine poetry came out of their 1920s revolt and a few great novels. But like everything else it faded back into itself. There would be more wars to come. More repeats. More re-runs. More of the same. It's what we do. What we've always done.

You may think we've travelled a long way from the myth of the Garden of Eden. But you'd be wrong. We've come no distance at all. We're always up against these discords:

. . . in the pact of things . . .
That singly hold, yet give the lie
To him who seeks to yoke them both—

For Nietzsche it was the discord or tension between the Apollonian and the Dionysian, the ordered world of reason versus the Dionysian itch for the transcendent. The need for order and control against the urge towards abandonment and the ecstasy and release it promised, a disjunction the scholars of the counterculture were well aware of. Joan Didion may have been the most insightful of the counter-culture's reporters, but Theodore Roszak, then Professor of History at California State University, was its most perceptive student. He saw it not as a tension between the Apollonian and the Dionysian so much as a conflict between the objective consciousness of science and the visionary imagination of mystics, seers and artists. However you describe the disjunction, it is important to remember that it is not necessarily one between science and religion. Religion can be just as Apollonian as science, especially in its cassocked and organised manifestation. It is always a need to control, a fear of disorder, a mistrust of freedom – and panic in the face of the Dionysian impulse towards rhapsody and excess. We caught a furtive glimpse of it in Christianity's hatred of sexuality, the most Dionysian of the human instincts. We heard William Blake's contempt for the priests in black gowns who were walking their rounds and binding with briars his joys and desires. But the Church wasn't Blake's only target. He found the same passion for order among scientists, their need to mansplain everything squeezing the mystery and magic out of the universe. He longed for them . . .

> To see a World in a Grain of Sand
> And a Heaven in a Wild Flower,
> Hold Infinity in the palm of your hand
> And Eternity in an hour

. . . the way he did. For Blake eighteenth-century Lambeth was teeming with 'visions buried in its stones and mortar waiting for their revelation'.[6] He and his wife Catherine had moved into 13 Hercules Buildings in the London borough of Lambeth in 1790, and it was there he had some of his most famous visions, available to us still in the paintings he left. Among them is the ink and water-colour painting of Newton, where the famous scientist is seen crouched over, binding all existence in an arc of regimented rationality that Blake described as 'Newton's sleep'. The same authoritarian conceit is evident in Blake's Ancient as, like Newton, he divides the cosmos into motion, heat and gravity.[7] Blake's Ancient is not God. It is Urizen, in Blakean mythology the embodiment of conventional reason and morality, usually depicted as a bearded old man ensnaring people in webs of law and convention, the personification of Reason and Science. Blake was as contemptuous of Apollonian religion as he was of Apollonian science.

'Well, so what?' we might mutter to ourselves; Blake

was a great artist, but a man who sees visions on the stairs in an ordinary house in south London is clearly out of his mind. Sorry, no. Just out of *your* mind. Definitely in his own mind. For, as Milton reminded us, the mind is its own place, the place through which all reality is mediated to us. So be careful how you respond to minds like Blake's or you might miss something. Roszak certainly wanted us to pay attention to him. He wanted us to admit the possibility that there are people like Blake who see the world not as commonplace sight or scientific scrutiny sees it, but who see it transformed and made lustrous, and in so seeing it see it as it really is.[8]

The basis of the scientific method is the conviction that the only way to gain reliable knowledge of external reality is by a process of critical enquiry cleansed of all subjective distortion and personal involvement. Roszak calls this way of looking at the world '*objective consciousness*', as opposed to the subjective or engaged consciousness of mystics like Blake.

> . . . objective consciousness is emphatically *not* some manner of definitive, transcultural development whose cogency derives from the fact that it is uniquely in touch with truth. Rather, like a mythology, it is an arbitrary construct in which a given society in a given historical situation has invested its sense of meaningfulness and value. And so, like any mythology, it can be . . . called into question by cultural movements which find meaning and value elsewhere.[9]

Roszak asks who we think we are when we are being purely objective. He wonders how we managed to bring this purely objective self into existence, and how we can be sure we have really pulled it off. It recalls Kuhn's point about the different ways we have of looking at the same thing. Or my point about the creativity we all bring to our interpretations of reality. As well as reading stories *out of* what we perceive, we read stories *into* what we perceive. We see things not as they are, but as we are. And how we do our reading has consequences. We have noticed the consequences for women in how Christians read the Adam and Eve story. We are now getting a clearer understanding of the dire consequences for the planet of the way we have also objectified and exploited nature for our own ends, as directed by God in Genesis when he told us to:

> . . . fill the earth and subdue it: and have dominion over the fish of the sea and over the birds of the air and over every living thing that moves upon the earth.[10]

Roszak anticipated the fatal damage this form of consciousness would wreak on the planet, the main casualty of our objective manipulations.

> An objective, meaning an alienated, attitude toward the natural environment comes easily these days to a population largely born and made in the almost totally man-made world of the metropolis. It would be difficult for anyone so raised, including a scientist, *not* to be objective toward a 'nature' which he has only known in the form of tidy, if boring, artificialities arranged by the parks and gardens authorities. The flora, fauna, landscape, and increasingly the climate of the earth lie

practically helpless at the feet of technological man, tragically vulnerable to his arrogance . . . we have triumphed over them . . . at least until the massive ecological consequences catch up with us.[11]

As well as anticipating the ecological crisis that has become catastrophic in our time, he foresaw the emergence of what scientists today are calling 'the technological singularity', a hypothetical point in the future when technological growth will become uncontrollable and irreversible, resulting in unfathomable changes to human civilisation – if it survives that long.

We may only have to wait until our fellow humans have converted themselves into purely impersonal automatons capable of total objectivity in all their tasks. At that point, when the mechanistic imperative has been successfully internalised as the prevailing life-style of our society, we shall find ourselves moving through a world of perfected bureaucrats, managers, operations analysts, and social engineers who will be indistinguishable from the cybernated systems they assist.[12]

Written in 1971, those words were prescient of the calamity that confronts the human community as I write these words in 2019, when the disjunctions of human consciousness are more pronounced and irreconcilable than ever. It is a deadly business, this inability to hear the other's story or to acknowledge that there may be other ways of responding to reality than our own. When Roszak was writing his book the man in the White House was a tightly wound Apollonian called Richard Nixon. Nixon had started his presidency in 1969, and many of his decisions were fuelled by a visceral contempt for the counterculture. In particular, he loathed its use of psychedelics and other drugs, the side of the counterculture that presented itself most conspicuously to those who chose not to look below its surface.

In outlawing acid, President Nixon kick-started his Apollonian 'war on drugs' – Vietnam aside, the most catastrophic of the decisions he made before his presidency ended in disgrace in 1974. The US finally left Vietnam in 1975 after three million Vietnamese and 58,000 members of the American military had been killed, but the war on drugs launched by Nixon shows no sign of ending. Like that other Apollonian experiment, Prohibition, it continues to enrich criminals and their lethal cartels, kill children, destroy national economies and paralyse the judgement centres in the brains of politicians everywhere. If only they'd learned how to read, the warning was laid out for them by the author of Genesis in the myth of the Garden of Eden, where God is the ruthlessly optimistic authoritarian figure who loves to ban things and thereby renders them irresistible.

> And the Lord God commanded the man, saying, 'You may freely eat of every tree of the garden; but of the tree of the knowledge of good and evil you shall not eat, for in the day that you eat of it you shall die.'[13]

Authoritarians are people who think they know how the rest of us should live and how we should be governed.

Never how we might learn to govern ourselves. *They* have the prescription that the rest of us just have to swallow. More potently, they know precisely what we should never be allowed to swallow, especially if they are euphoric substances that might lead us into Dionysian excesses and ecstasies. *For in the day that you eat of it you shall die* – the motto of every puritanical regime in history that ever tried to force people into the perfect template it had designed for them. They always hate and mistrust human freedom, the knowledge of good and evil. And they never learn from the cruelty that is always the consequence of the plan they have for the rest of us. They have the formula that will cure us of ourselves, if we'll but submit to the *gnosis* revealed unto them. And if we won't submit, well then, they'll make us, these ruthless optimists who know what's good for the rest of us. Which is why we never learn and go on repeating the same mistakes, ideological recidivists.

History is a continuous narrative in which one action leads fatally on to another. A butterfly flaps its wings in South America and results in a tsunami in Southeast Asia. A paranoid President's hatred of promiscuous kids on a San Francisco street getting high on acid in 1970 leads to the death of an alienated twelve-year-old-kid from London, a pawn in a county-line drug deal in 2019. Stories connect. Knit together. Even if the connections are oppositional and link only in disagreement and disjunction. That's why learning how to read history is our clearest imperative still. And the one we find the toughest to achieve. Psychedelics were always about more than getting high. They were also, in Roszak's words, about seeing the world transformed and made lustrous beyond measure.

Lysergic acid diethylamide, LSD, was an accidental invention, a molecule first synthesised by a scientist called Albert Hofmann in 1938. Hofmann had been looking for a drug to stimulate circulation, but when he accidentally ingested a tiny quantity of the new chemical, he realised he had created something 'at once terrifying and wondrous'.[14] Another molecule had been around for 5,000 years doing the same sort of thing, this one produced not by a chemist, 'but by a little brown mushroom . . . which would come to be known as psilocybin'. It had been used by the indigenous peoples of Mexico and Central America as a sacrament, till it was suppressed by the Roman Catholic Church after the Spanish conquest – *you shall not eat, for in the day that you eat of it you shall die.* Of course, they did continue to eat of it, secretly, illegally, as always happens when the powers that have assumed authority over us order us how to live. Twelve years after Hofmann's discovery of LSD, an amateur mycologist called R. Gordon Wasson sampled these sacramental mushrooms while on a visit to Mexico, and described them in 1957 in *Life* magazine as causing 'strange visions'. In the 1950s and early 1960s LSD and psilocybin were seen by the psychiatric establishment as miracle drugs for the treatment of a number of disorders, including anxiety, alcoholism and depression.[15]

These were the molecules that became the sacrament of the counterculture that was so hated by President Nixon, because they were sapping America's young of the willingness to fight in the country's wars. According to Stanislav Grof, Nixon suppressed research into psychedelics because they had loosed a Dionysian element into America in the 1960s, and were threatening the country's puritan values.[16] Self-authenticating mystical experiences have always been threatening to existing hierarchical structure; it's the same old tension between Dionysus and Apollo that never goes away. But I am less interested in the politics of psychedelics and the history of their suppression than in what they might teach us about other ways of seeing the world. This is how Barbara Ehrenreich expressed the challenge:

> Maybe our animist ancestors were on to something that we have lost sight of in the last few hundred years of rigid monotheism, science, and Enlightenment. And that is the insight that the natural world is not dead, but swarming with activity, sometimes perhaps even agency and intentionality. Even the place where you might expect to find quiet and solidity, the very heart of matter – the interior of a proton or a neutron – turns out to be animated with the ghostly flickerings of quantum fluctuations.[17]

Though he was too timid to try psychedelics himself, the scholar who knew most about these mystical experiences and wrote about them most sympathetically was the American psychologist William James. It was in Edinburgh in the years 1901–2 that he delivered his Gifford Lectures, subsequently published as the book *Varieties of Religious Experience: A Study in Human Nature*. Lectures XVI and XVII were on Mysticism:

> . . . mystical states seem to those who experience them to be also states of knowledge. They are states of insight

into depths unplumbed by the discursive intellect. They are illuminations, revelations, full of significance and importance, all inarticulate though they remain; and as a rule they carry with them a curious sense of authority for after-time.[18]

As I've said, though James never himself experimented with any of the substances that could provoke these mystical states, he was well aware of the claims made for them, as well as of the attempts by authority to suppress them.

The next step into mystical states carries us into a realm that public opinion and ethical philosophy have long since branded as pathological, though private practice and certain lyrical strains of poetry seem still to bear witness to its ideality . . . Nitrous oxide and ether, especially nitrous oxide, when sufficiently diluted with air, stimulate the mystical consciousness in an extraordinary degree. Depth beyond depth of truth seems revealed to the inhaler.[19]

He tells us that he'd made some observations on nitrous oxide intoxication and reported them in print. The main conclusion that was forced upon his mind by his observations remained unshaken. This is what he wrote:

It is that normal waking consciousness, rational consciousness as we call it, is but one special type of consciousness, whilst all about it, parted from it by the filmiest of screens, there lie potential forms of consciousness entirely different. We may go through life without suspecting their existence; but apply the requisite stimulus, and at a touch they are there in all their completeness, definite types of mentality which probably somewhere have their field of application and adaptation. No account of the universe in its totality can be final which leaves these forms of consciousness quite disregarded . . . *At any rate, they forbid a premature closing of our accounts with reality.*[20]

I put that last sentence in italics because it jumped out at Michael Pollan when he started researching psychedelics for his recent book, *How to Change Your Mind*. He tells us that 'The first time I read that sentence, I realized James had my number: as a staunch materialist, and as an adult of a certain age, I had pretty much closed my accounts with reality. Perhaps this had been premature. Well, here was an invitation to reopen them'.[21] Which is exactly what his fascinating book does – and in a way that does not bully or force us to take a particular line on the subject. One of the things I admired about his book is the way it exemplifies a generous and ecumenical way of reading human history and its struggles with meaning. He tells us that while it had never occurred to Hofmann that his discovery would become a 'pleasure drug', he also

. . . came to regard the youth culture's adoption of LSD in the 1960s as an understandable response to the emptiness of what he described as a materialistic, industrialized, and spiritually impoverished society that had lost its connection to nature. This master of chemistry . . . emerged from his experience with LSD-25 convinced the molecule offered civilization not only a potential therapeutic but also a spiritual balm – by opening a crack 'in the edifice of materialistic rationality'.[22]

What I liked most about Pollan's book was the way it refused to shunt us into either of the dead ends that always face us when we debate the possible meanings of the universe. It might just be a material reality that is entirely its own thing, with no depth of meaning or purpose beyond it. Or it might be a sacrament that mediates another, transcendent reality to us. Yet another of those antisyzygys that won't let us rest securely at either end. The mind-altering power of psilocybin could point to an entirely materialist understanding of consciousness, because the changes in the mind it produces can be traced directly to the action of a chemical. But the fact remains that even the most secular of the people who experienced those changes became convinced they transcended a purely material understanding of reality and pointed to something beyond. Pollan writes:

> If the experience of transcendence is mediated by molecules that flow through both our brains and the natural world of plants and fungi, then perhaps nature is not as mute as Science has told us, and 'Spirit', however defined, exists *out there* . . .[23]

Pollan takes several pages to describe his own experience of ingesting the little brown mushrooms. He doesn't overplay the experience either, and isn't quite sure what to make of it. It was definitely a spiritual encounter. He felt the personhood of other beings, including 'the damn bugs on our property', and he had an experience of wonder and immanence that transformed his familiar world into something numinous. What I appreciate most about his account is his refusal to jump to an absolute conclusion on the nature of what happened to him. Here he is again:

> Before this afternoon, I had always assumed access to a spiritual dimension hinged on one's acceptance of the supernatural – of God, of a Beyond – but now I'm not so sure. The Beyond, whatever it consists of, might not be nearly as far away or inaccessible as we think . . . But if these dried-up little scraps of fungus taught me anything, it is that there are other, stranger forms of consciousness available to us, and, whatever they mean, their very existence, to quote William James again, 'forbids a premature closing of our accounts with reality'.[24]

Isn't that the wisest and the sanest posture to adopt towards the mystery of our own being, as well as the being of being itself? To live with the tension of opposing truths 'without any irritable reaching after fact and reason'. I've always thought that the most powerful word in Keats's famous celebration of uncertainty in his theory of Negative Capability is *irritable*, with its root in the Latin for anger, the engine that propels most of our intrusions into the lives of others. It is certainly there in the exasperation that comes off the authoritarian personality like a steam, as it orders us to get in line and follow the programme it has decreed for our salvation. It is irritable, because it closed its accounts with reality ages ago, knows exactly what history is up to, and is furious with us for refusing to follow its route map to the Promised Land.

That kind of anger is a giveaway, a sign of insecurity, a fear that our certainties are not as secure as we'd like them to be. And it can make us punishers and persecutors. Unable to live with the suspicion that we may not actually be in possession of the final truth, we punish others for owning what we cannot admit in ourselves: the presence of doubt. A fundamental test of the worth of our stories is their effect on others, so the questions we should ask ourselves are: if I choose to believe and try to live by this story, what will be its consequences for the lives of others? What will its fruits be? Will it make me a despiser and divider, maybe even a persecutor of others, a killer? If so, why all this rage? Where is it coming from and what is it trying to tell us? Like the chest pain that signals an impending heart attack, rage is a sign that violent certainty is a danger to our spiritual health. It blocks the flow of our relationship with others. That's why the mystics advise us that there are kinder ways of apprehending reality than through the official channels of organised religion. And there are always more mystics around than we imagine.

VII

MYSTICISM WITHOUT
MUSHROOMS

Psilocybin – magic mushrooms – and other psyche-delics may have been the portal to the mystical state in Central American culture, but they do not seem to figure much in the history of European or eastern mysticism. Here mystical states are induced by other means. Some of them are the result of intense ascetical practices and methods of prayer; others seem to hit the participant out of nowhere like a sudden visitation. It may say something about the decline of Christianity in the West that the average person in the street, if interested in the phenom-enon at all, is more likely to be aware of the traditions and methods of Eastern mysticism than of their European Christian counterparts. The obvious example is the popu-larity of yoga in the West. Even if it is only practised as a means to physical health and wellbeing, it always comes tinged with something deeper than the ability to place the body in a series of extraordinary positions. When I prac-tised it seriously years ago, the physical sessions always ended with a meditation conducted by the leader, clearly aimed at opening the minds of the practitioners to some kind of spiritual illumination.

In India, yoga's birthplace, Hindu adepts used it to

discipline their minds and senses, in order to overcome their human limitations and identify their individual selves with the undifferentiated 'eternal self'. After a practice based on exercise, diet, posture, breathing, concentration and moral discipline, the yogi would enter a state of release called *samādhi*.

> Holding his body steady with the three upper parts erect, and causing the senses with the mind to enter into the heart, a wise man with the Brahma-boat should cross over all the fear-bringing streams. Having repressed his breathings here in the body, and having his movements checked, one should breathe through his nostrils with diminished breath . . . His mind the wise man should restrain undistractedly . . . A practiser of Yoga beholds here the nature of Brahma (Creator), unborn, steadfast, from every nature free . . .[1]

> The precept for effecting this (unity) is this: restraint of the breath, withdrawal of the senses, meditation, concentration, contemplation, absorption. Such is said to be the six-fold Yoga. By this means when a seer sees the brilliant Maker, Lord, Person, the Brahma-source, then, being a knower, shaking off good and evil, he reduces everything to unity in the supreme Imperishable.[2]

In *Varieties of Religious Experience* William James describes the intense praxis used by Buddhists to achieve a similar state of release, though *dhyāna* is the word they use for these higher states of contemplation. He describes four stages in achieving *dhyāna*.

The first stage comes through the concentration of the mind upon one point. It excludes desire, but not discernment or judgment ... In the second stage the intellectual function drops off, and the satisfied sense of unity remains. In the third stage the satisfaction departs, and indifference begins ... In the fourth stage the indifference, memory, and self-consciousness are perfected.[3]

Even higher stages of contemplation are hinted at, where nothing exists, neither ideas nor the absence of ideas. The illusory nature of this world, and the desire for escape by those trapped in it, is the key to the metaphysic implicit in both Hinduism and Buddhism. Human souls are caught on the wheel of *samsāra*, or passing through, as existence follows existence, until the soul, purged of desire and illusion, is blown out like a candle and released into the bliss of non-being, like a river pouring itself into the sea.

One of the interesting aspects of the mystical experience is that on one level the participants appear to conform themselves to the particular religious tradition to which they belong, but at another, higher level it transcends the theological traditions of the participants. One way of expressing this is to acknowledge that while there may be many paths up a mountain, they all merge on to the peak at the top.

If I am walking on the side of a mountain I can see first a lake, then after a few steps a forest. I have to choose either the lake or the forest. If I want to see both lake and forest at once, I have to climb higher.[4]

That's why William James said the classics of mysticism had 'neither birthday nor native land'. This may become clearer when we turn to the most famous of the Christian mystics, the Spanish Carmelite nun, Saint Teresa of Avila (1515–82). The technical term the Catholic mystics used to describe their method of contemplation or meditation was 'orison'. Here is Saint Teresa describing her own experiences:

> In the orison of union the soul is fully awake as regards God, but wholly asleep as regards things of this world and in respect of herself. During the short time the union lasts, she is as it were deprived of every feeling, and even if she would, she could not think of any single thing. Thus she needs to employ no artifice in order to arrest the use of her understanding: it remains so stricken with inactivity that she neither knows what she loves, nor in what manner she loves, nor what she wills. In short, she is utterly dead to the things of the world and lives solely in God . . . I do not even know whether in this state she has enough life left to breathe. It seems to me she has not; or at least that if she does breathe, she is unaware of it. Her intellect would fain understand something of what is going on within her, but it has so little force now that it can act in no way whatsoever. So a person who falls into a deep faint appears as dead . . . Thus does God, when he raises a soul to union with himself, suspend the natural action of all her faculties. She neither sees, hears, nor understands, so long as she is united with God . . . God establishes himself in the interior of this soul in such

a way, that when she returns to herself, it is wholly impossible for her to doubt that she has been in God and God in her.[5]

That description of the experience of mystical union could fit almost any theological or spiritual tradition, yet on another day Teresa tells us that while she was reciting the Athanasian Creed:

Our Lord made me comprehend in what way it is that one God can be in three Persons. He made me see it so clearly that I remained as extremely surprised as I was comforted . . . and now, when I think of the Holy Trinity, or hear It spoken of, I understand how the three adorable Persons form only one God and I experience an unspeakable happiness.[6]

Am I mistaken in detecting a note of impatience in that exclamation? *Surprised* as well as comforted? Surprised at what? That the doctrine of the Trinity can be made sense of? Maybe there is a hint of that kind of surprise here. If there is, it would explain why religious authorities – particularly in Christianity – have always been concerned about the orthodoxy of their mystics, whom they suspect of sitting lightly to their authorised and exclusive route maps for the ascent to God, not to mention their official description of what it will be like when we get there. It does seem to be the case that the further up the mountain they go and the nearer to God they get, the less mystics believe any human formulation can capture the nature of the divine mystery. For them, God is always beyond symbols, concepts, metaphors and analogies; in fact, beyond human language. In both the Eastern and Western mystical traditions, the divine is never *this*, or even *like* this; it is always *not this*, or *not like* this.

In Christian mysticism this way of talking about God in negatives is called 'apophatic' theology, from the Greek for *deny* or *negate*. We can never say what God *is*, only what God is *not* – and that includes *anything* we try to say about the divine mystery. The danger that always faces us when we start thinking or talking about God is *idolatry*. Not idol in the sense of a little image formed out of wood or clay, but idol in the sense of a human construct *of any sort*, even a form of words – *particularly a form of words: God in our image, a projection of our thoughts or desires or secret revenges.* And doesn't our history support and confirm that anxiety? Isn't it littered with the tombstones of the gods we made in our own image, till they died of our embarrassment or we ourselves euthanised them? Let me identify a few of them. Here is the god who demanded that we sacrifice our bulls and goats to him and the first fruits of all our crops. Here is the god for whom that was not enough, and demanded the sacrifice of our children as well. Over there is the god who told us that 'if a male lies with a male as with a woman . . . they shall be put to death'. And in that corner, behind the curtain of faded brocade, lurks the god who commanded us to drown witches and burn heretics. When you come to think of it, we are all atheists now, because we all have gods we no longer believe in, gods we have sent to the graveyard, even if there is *one* we still hold on to. That's why good-humoured people who have abandoned *all* the gods sometimes josh believers in God with the crack, we are all atheists now, it's just that I disbelieve in one more god than you.

It is in that sense that real mystics are also atheistic. They so fear the human capacity for idolatry, for making god in our own image – and the horrors and cruelties that too easily follow that self-identification – that they refuse to accept *any* of our descriptions or definitions of God. They warn us that if we must talk about God at all we can only do it in negatives. We can only say what God is *not*, never what God *is*, an approach that is classically associated with an early Christian mystic from around 500 CE, known as Pseudo-Dionysius the Areopagite. To the point of tedium, Dionysius hammered away at the negatives:

> The cause of all things is neither soul nor intellect; nor has it imagination, opinion, or reason, or intelligence; nor is it reason or intelligence; nor is it spoken or thought . . . It is neither essence, nor eternity, nor time . . . it is neither science nor truth. It is not even royalty or wisdom; not one; not unity; not divinity . . .[7]

You can see why the uniformed branch of the Church hated that kind of thing. How could you get the faithful to conform to something as nebulous as that? How could you persuade them that if they did not buy it their souls would be in danger of eternal damnation? Because there was literally *nothing* definite for them to get hold of. It would never work. Authorities need the smack of firm doctrine. Words they can drill into the minds of believers. Formulas they can test people on and punish them for any deviations from the truth *as defined by them*, the mark of ruthless optimists everywhere, with their infallible cure for what ails us.

No wonder they were suspicious of mystics and preferred to lock them up rather than have them wandering around unsettling the lives of the pious. That was certainly what they tried to do to the mystic Meister Eckhart (1260–1328), a German theologian and member of the Dominican Order. Like Dionysius, Eckhart talked of the still desert of the Godhead, 'where never was seen difference, neither Father, Son, nor Holy Ghost, where there is no one at home, yet where the spark of the soul is more at peace than in itself.'[8] Accused of heresy in 1326, tried before the Archbishop of Cologne and knowing what a guilty verdict would have entailed, Eckhart was probably fortunate to die during the proceedings that had been brought against him.

Is it possible to have any sympathy with these authorities and their anxious certainties? This, I suppose, can be said: whenever a spiritual revelation is enshrined in an institution invented to carry its meaning through time, it is easy to understand how its guardians can become overprotective of the treasure they are responsible for, especially if their access to the original vision is theoretical rather than experiential, something they *read* about, rather than something they know directly. It may be the difference between talent and genius, the gap between Salieri and Mozart. Or maybe it is evidence, deep down, of the abyss of doubt we are all afraid to look into lest whatever frail beliefs we possess evaporate. Wherever it comes from, there is a clear tendency in subsequent generations of believers to overdefine and concretise the original revelation. And to divinise or come close to divinising the one to whom the original revelation came. Incidentally, we find the same dynamic at work in the field of political revelations. Which is why Marxist-Leninism, Maoism and Fascism all have the same characteristics as fanatical religious movements, the same tendency to deify their founders and dear leaders, the same brutal intolerance of doctrinal dissidents, and the same capacity for brutal authoritarianism.

Is it possible to have any sympathy for this tendency towards absolutism in human affairs, this lust or need for *certainty*, whether religious or political? A wary sympathy, perhaps. An understanding of the insecurity that provokes the need, maybe. But a fear of it, nevertheless. No, a fear of *ourselves*, because we know what we are capable of doing to each other when we are possessed by these convictions. We know where these absolute commitments can lead us. The betrayals they can provoke, even among members of the same family. The knock on the door at 2 a.m. The disappearances. The long silences. The ones no longer spoken about. All because something in us is easily seduced by the idea of the idol who demands absolute allegiance in return for absolute security. Most betrayals in history are rooted in versions of that need. Which is why it is possible to sympathise with it and utterly to fear it in the same moment, knowing the sorrows and hates it can provoke.

And the turning of God into this idol, this absolute version of *ourselves*, was what the best of the mystics feared as well. 'Neither is this Thou,' they would say, anxious in case they trapped themselves in an absolutised version of themselves. In that sense they were all *a-theists*. God was never *this*. Always *not this, nor that*. No wonder they frustrated the religious organisation types, the ones who ran the institutions that had solved the God problem and the God longing, and wanted to keep it going and growing. They knew doubt didn't sell. Doubt made people anxious. People wanted to *know*, wanted certainty – whether religious or political. Wanted to be *sure*. Who doesn't sympathise with that longing, that need? But think where it can lead us? Think of all the heavens that turned into hell. Think of all the absolutisms of the twentieth century and where they led us. The gods that failed. Because that's what gods do. *Fail.* They always fail. And to repeat the paradox: this is why the men and women who might, just *might* have encountered the True God – *if such exists* – are most afraid of all the other gods, the idol-gods made in our various images, not only because they are not God – *a-theos* – but because they are *us* enlarged and absolutised – our own worst nightmare.

Another aspect of mysticism the organised religions hated was its ecumenism, its refusal to allow God to be branded or owned by a particular denomination. Whatever the ecclesiastical authorities made of it, William James was convinced that the great achievement of mysticism was that it was an experience that transcended all times, places and traditions.

This is the everlasting and triumphant mystical tradition, hardly altered by differences of clime or creed . . . so that there is about mystical utterances an eternal unanimity which ought to make a critic stop and think, and which brings it about that the mystical classics have . . . neither birthday nor native land. Perpetually telling of the unity of man with God, their speech antedates languages, and they do not grow old.[9]

And they do not grow old. By now my readers may be doubting that. Living in the secular West, for them mystical experiences are as dead and done with as crinolines and horse-drawn taxis. But they'd be wrong. So, before trying to assess the significance of the kind of mystical experiences I've been describing, let me offer a couple of examples from our own era. The first one comes from the English writer, F.C. Happold.

It happened in my room in Peterhouse on the evening of February 1st, 1913, when I was an undergraduate at Cambridge. If I say that Christ came to me, I should be using conventional words which would carry no precise meaning; for Christ comes to men and women in different ways. When I tried to record the experience at the time, I used the imagery of the vision of the Holy Grail; it seemed to me to be like that. There was, however, no sensible vision. There was just the room, with its shabby furniture and the fire burning in the grate and the red-shaded lamp on the table. But the room was filled by a Presence, which in a strange way was both about me and within me, like light or warmth. I was overwhelmingly possessed by Someone who was not myself, and yet I felt more myself than I had ever been before. I was filled with intense happiness, and almost unbearable joy, such as I had never known before and have never known since. And over all was a deep sense of peace and security and certainty.

The other comes from the Scottish poet Edwin Muir. Before the beginning of the Second World War he was living in Saint Andrews in a state of despair that grew worse when his wife had to enter a nursing home.

I was returning from the nursing home one day – it was the last day of February 1939 – when I saw some schoolboys playing at marbles on the pavement; the old game had 'come round' again at its own time, known only to children, and it seemed a little rehearsal for a resurrection, promising a timeless renewal of life. I wrote in my diary next day: 'Last night, going to bed alone, I suddenly found myself (I was taking off my waistcoat) reciting the Lord's Prayer in a loud, emphatic voice – a thing I had not done for many years – with deep urgency and profound disturbed emotion. While I went on, I grew more composed; as if it had been empty and craving and were being replenished, my soul grew still; every word had a strange fullness of meaning which astonished and delighted me. It was late; I had sat up reading; I was sleepy; but as I stood in the midst of the floor, half-undressed, saying the prayer over and over, meaning after meaning sprang from it, overwhelming me again with joyful surprise; and I realized that this simple petition was always universal and always inexhaustible, and day by day sanctified human life.'

On the Richter scale of mystical experiences neither of these was particularly spectacular, yet each had a profound and life-changing effect on the subjects. And episodes like them keep happening in the lives of men and women we never hear of. This is what prompted the scientist Sir Alister Hardy to set up the Religious Experience Research Centre in 1969 to compile a database of spiritual and religious experiences like the ones just described. Hardy died in 1985, but the trust he established continues its work from a base in the University of Wales in Lampeter.

Hardy was a marine biologist and an expert on marine ecosystems, who became Linacre Professor of Zoology in the University of Oxford in 1946, a post he held till 1961. He was a Darwinian with a difference, one who added a twist of his own to evolutionary theory. He wondered whether something like telepathy might not have influenced the processes of evolution. He wondered whether certain animals might not share some kind of 'group mind', which he described as a 'sort of psychic blueprint between members of a species'. Might not all species, he suggested, be linked together in a 'cosmic mind' that was capable of carrying evolutionary information through time and space? Hardy was well aware that his views on spirituality would be scorned by members of the scientific community, which is why he kept them to himself till he retired from Oxford, knowing how scornful the scientific priesthood can be towards the heterodox and heretical. But he did not park the scientific method outside when exploring religious experiences of the mystical sort. He brought the spirit of scientific enquiry to his research much the way William James had brought it to his enquiries.

He thought of his research as an exercise in human ecology, a study of the human experience of contact with a personal power or purpose that was greater than, lay beyond, yet produced definite feelings in the individual self. He asked those who participated in his research: have you ever been aware of or influenced by a presence or power, whether you call it God or not, which is different from your everyday self? The archive that resulted contained accounts of the mystical experiences of 6,500 people.

It's hard to be absolutely sure how Hardy himself interpreted these experiences. My guess is that he thought they were beyond any absolute definition. He was sure they had biological roots, but he refused to reduce them to biology alone. He claimed that they had veridical authority for those who had experienced them. They pointed to a reality beyond themselves, but what was it?[10] I suspect he would have agreed with William James that, whatever you make of these mystical experiences, 'they forbid a premature closing of our accounts with reality'.

I don't know if Alister Hardy was aware of the work of the American sociologists Andrew M. Greeley and William C. McCready, but he would have been interested in what they were up to in the US in the 1970s had he come across it. Like Hardy, Greeley and McCready were interested in mystical experiences. Almost by accident, they had discovered that a number of people they knew had had encounters like the ones described by Happold and Muir. Curious, they made room in a 'representational national survey of ultimate values' among Americans they were embarking on at the time, and polled 1,500 adults with some questions on mystical experiences. The response staggered them. About 600 respondents reported having at least one such experience. In an attempt to identify the kind of people who were having them, they undertook a second survey and reported in 1974.

Who are the ones who have 'mystical' experiences? People in their 40s and 50s are somewhat more likely to report 'mystical' interludes than those in their 70s or their teens. Protestants are more likely to experience them than Jews, and Jews more likely than Catholics. Within the Protestant denominations, it is not the fundamentalists who are the most frequent 'mystics' but the Episcopalians (more than half of them). And within the two major denominational groups, the Irish are more likely than their co-religionists (be they Protestant or Catholic) to be mystical. Who are those who have these episodes often? They are disproportionately male, disproportionately black, disproportionately college-educated . . . and disproportionately Protestant.[11]

I've had several of these experiences myself. Though I would not place them very high on the mystical register, I'll recount two of them. The first happened when I was a curate in Glasgow in 1960, in the famous Citizens' Theatre, during a performance of their annual pantomime. The last scene of the panto was an impressionistic tableau of life in Glasgow, a typical day, from dawn to dusk. It began with workers going off early to the shipyards – they still had them in those days – moving down the dark streets, drawing on the first cigarette of the day. Then came the cleaning women with their mops and pails, making for the big offices in the city. Followed by paper boys and milk boys doing their early rounds. Next came children trudging to school. Then attractive young secretaries, followed by men with briefcases, wearing bowler hats, the day's *Glasgow Herald* tucked under their arms. On it went, till I had my moment of vision. I was no longer in the theatre. I was outside, floating above the city, observing it as a great ballet, with everything in its place, everything intended, everything part of the meaning and rhythm of the whole created universe. I wanted to embrace everyone and tell them about the unity of it all and their own part in it, the moves only they could make. I wanted them to know it all meant something, something beautiful, so they should no longer be defensive and afraid, no matter their suffering – they should be glad.

The second experience was not unlike the first. I was hurrying down Shaftesbury Avenue in London one afternoon years later, late for a meeting, when everything went into slow motion. Before I crossed this particular threshold, everything was rushed and untidy, without direction, a meaningless jostle of people and buses and traffic policemen. But over the threshold, into the experience, the moment the slow-motion switch was thrown, everything changed. Again, it was a ballet I witnessed, a pattern I perceived. The traffic policeman was conducting a great dance and every part was spontaneous yet arranged. Nothing was without meaning, yet everything was free. I wanted to embrace it all and have it all embraced, because we were a great company, a dance company, a family ballet, not a crowd of strangers. Why couldn't everyone see that? I saw it in a flash, and continued my way down the street grinning affectionately at everyone I passed.

I have often wondered about these experiences, and one or two others I've had. Not experiences of God, but of the world transfigured. More words from Edwin Muir, who would have understood:

Was it a vision?
Or did we see that day the unseeable
One glory of the everlasting world
Perpetually at work, though never seen
Since Eden locked the gate that's everywhere
And nowhere?[12]

Whatever you make of these claims to mystical experience, the high-flown as well as the down-to-earth, they leave us with the question of what level of authority and truth we can attribute to them? What is going on when they happen? And what are we to make of it? An answer in three parts suggests itself.

First, we have to acknowledge that mystical experiences are clearly authoritative for the individuals who have them. We can recognise that, while also acknowledging at the same time that no authority emanates from them that can compel the assent of those who stand outside them. This is an important qualification that religious authorities find it hard to accept. Though religious authority is wary of mystics once their faith system has been institutionally developed, it usually acknowledges that it was the mystical experiences of the religion's founder that prompted the formation of the system in the first place. Sadly, its leaders are never content to say, *we* believe in what our founder has seen and heard, and it compels our obedience. We realise that it may not carry the same authority for you, but please respect our belief and accord it your tolerance. Most religious traditions go much further than that. They commit a sleight-of-hand that transforms their statements of faith into scientific claims with the authority of provable fact. In Scruton's language, faith is *'scientized'*. Some of them go further than that, as we have seen, and claim that *unless you also believe, you'll be damned everlastingly.*

So there's a stand-off. The arguments roll. And neither side really listens to the other. But we don't have to stay stuck in this stand-off. While refusing to accord mystical experiences the kind of universal authority religion claims for them, we could acknowledge that there may be other forms of consciousness than the rationalistic ones we prefer or have ourselves only ever experienced. We could admit that they carry an implicit authority for those who have experienced them. And at the minimum, we could acknowledge that they open out the *possibility* of other orders of truth and ways to access it. William James offered this reflection on the subject:

One conclusion was forced upon my mind at that time, and my impression of its truth has ever since remained unshaken. It is that our normal waking consciousness, rational consciousness . . . is but one special type of consciousness, whilst all about it, parted from it by the filmiest of screens, there lie potential forms of consciousness entirely different. We may go through life without suspecting their existence; but apply the requisite stimulus, and at a touch they are there in all their completeness, definite types of mentality which probably somewhere have their field of application and adaptation . . . they all converge towards a kind of insight to which I cannot help ascribing some metaphysical significance. The keynote of it is invariably a reconciliation. It is as if the opposites of the world, whose contradictoriness and conflict make all our difficulties and troubles, were melted into unity.[13]

Is that where we have to leave it, then? In what one of my teachers described as 'an equilibrium of mutual dissatisfaction', a permanent stand-off between professional oppositionists, totally committed to their end of the dispute? I think it is too important to leave this stand-off to the professionals. Here I want to recall words I have already quoted from Jonathan Rée's book, *Witcraft: The Invention of Philosophy in English*. He noticed how professionals treated philosophy as their exclusive domain, so that the history of philosophy became the story of their opinions and interactions with each other over the centuries. He wrote:

. . . the historians of philosophy have carried on as before, repeating familiar stories about the little band of philosophers who have become mainstays of modern textbooks . . . they have continued to ignore all the other people who have tried to understand the world in the light of philosophy and who were, as often as not, transformed by the experience . . . It gave them the courage to ask their own questions about how the world works and how they should lead their lives. It opened their minds and set them free . . .[14]

That applies with even greater force in disputes about the ultimate meaning of existence, a subject we cannot leave to professional disputants on either side of this ancient argument, whether rationalists or believers. Interestingly, some professional participants in the contest are beginning to rethink their approach as well. One of them is the philosopher Julian Baggini, an atheist who is beginning to search for a more ecumenical way through the stand-off. Here's what he writes in his latest global history of philosophy:

> Secular reason has been a powerful tool for scientific and intellectual development. But complacency about its benefits needs to be challenged, perhaps by traditions that have maintained that philosophy and science exist only to serve human flourishing. If our ultimate goal is human good, the autonomy of reason alone cannot be absolute. Who would want to build and stock the finest libraries in the world without caring if they stand amidst desolate streets?[15]

Baggini also turns to William James for help. Not to the expert on mysticism and religious experience. This time he turns to James the exponent of pragmatism, an American school of philosophy whose founders, in addition to James, were John Dewey and Charles Sanders Peirce. Here's Baggini again:

Pragmatism's philosophical lineage extends back to British empiricism. The nineteenth-century philosopher and psychologist William James explicitly linked pragmatism to 'the great English way of investigating a conception' which is 'to ask yourself right off, "What is it *known as*? In what facts does it result?"'

James's definition echoes those given by two other great founders of pragmatism, John Dewey and Charles Sanders Peirce. Peirce defined the central principle of pragmatism as follows: 'Consider what effects, that might conceivably have practical bearings, we conceive of our conception to have. Then our conception of these effects is the whole of our conception of the object.' Similarly, Dewey wrote that 'knowledge is always a matter of the use that is made of experienced natural events' and that 'knowing is a way of employing empirical occurrences with respect to increasing power to direct the consequences which flow from things' . . .

Pragmatism takes abstractions such as truth and meaning and links them to human action. 'The essence of belief is the establishment of a habit . . . and different beliefs are distinguished by the different modes of action to which they give rise . . . What a thing means is simply what habits it involves'.[16]

Beliefs are rules for *action*, and the whole function of thinking is but one step in the production of habits of action. One consequence of adopting the pragmatist viewpoint is that, in Baggini's words, 'many philosophical problems are not so much *solved* as *dissolved*':

. . . many traditional metaphysical problems . . . are shown to be pseudo-problems that arose only because philosophers got lost in clouds of confusion thrown up by concepts that they had erroneously detached from the world of lived experience. The search for ultimate causes and explanations is a futile one . . . As Dewey wrote, 'Philosophy recovers itself when it ceases to be a device for dealing with the problems of philosophers and becomes a method, cultivated by philosophers, for dealing with the problems of men.'[17]

It was in this sense that for William James religious beliefs *worked* or, as he put it, they had 'cash value'. They gave people meaning, purpose, values and a sense of belonging. And they often prompted them to heroic service of others. Does it matter what the story is if it can encourage such sacrifice?

Early in January 1990, I was sent by Christian Aid on a fact-finding mission to El Salvador at the height of the bloody civil war that was raging there. I was driven round the country in an armoured vehicle with an armed guard to assess what was going on. On one unforgettable day I visited the Jesuit's Pastoral Centre at the University of Central America only hours after an army death squad had gunned down eight of them in their residence because of their opposition to the vicious regime. The corridors were still streaked with blood and the wall against which the six Jesuits and their two assistants had been executed was peppered with bullet holes. I met members of other Catholic religious orders putting their lives on the line every day in their opposition to the murderous regime. As

William James the pragmatist would have put it, the cash value of their religious faith was heroism, self-sacrifice and the service of others, even unto death. In that context, did it really matter what their precise parsing of the doctrine of the Holy Trinity or the nature of the presence of Christ in the Eucharist might have been?

The difficulty with the pragmatic approach to religion – that beliefs are just rules for action or that the essence of belief is the establishment of habit – is that it is not what believers think they are doing when they are believing and acting. They understand their actions to be the direct consequence of their beliefs. They do not say: in order to perform these actions or establish these habits I have decided to believe these things. It is always the other way around. They say: I believe this or that to be the case, and the direct consequence of this belief is the impulsion to establish these habits or to follow these rules.

How are we to negotiate these different perspectives? Does it boil down to personal psychology? I wonder, for example, if William James's resort to the pragmatic justification of religious belief may have been rooted in his temperament. He was fascinated by religion and felt a generalised warmth towards it, but was unable to commit himself to any particular belief, just as he was fascinated by psychedelics but never dared try them himself. Did he admire commitment in others because he found it lacking in himself, much the way a person suffering from tone-deafness may admire another's perfect pitch? I don't know, but it doesn't seem unlikely. I've known quite a few people who have said to me, I don't believe in God but I wish I could. Belief can give structure, direction and meaning to a person – a story to live by. These are the *concomitants* of faith, not its rationale, and they can provoke longing in people who lack them. But is the longing for the *belief*, or for its concomitants, the security it seems to bring? Hard to say, but it is an interesting dialectic.

In the case of Julian Baggini, I wonder if his interest in the pragmatic approach to these issues may not be rooted in his intellectual generosity and desire to seek alliances with religious believers for the common good. He is both baffled and impressed by the religious philosophies of the Eastern tradition, with their openness to mystical or intuitive methods of apprehending reality, in contrast to the West's emphasis on rationality as the only route to the truth. But what do you do if you are a rationalist who is aware of the damage an exclusively rationalist approach to life can do to humanity and the earth it inhabits? And how are you to respond if you see the benefits to society and human flourishing of metaphysical beliefs you cannot share? The wisest approach is to remember William James's advice, and refuse a premature closing of your accounts with reality. You learn to look both ways.

Another attractive version of pragmatism came from the American philosopher, the late Richard Rorty. Rorty, a generous-minded atheist, was more interested in the impact of a belief on human flourishing than in its origins. If it was a good idea, if it helped humanity, why did it matter what had motivated it, or what its origins were? He offered Nietzsche as an example. Nietzsche had been interested in what he called 'The Genealogy of Morals', their origins in humanity's deep past. A noble idea could have an ignoble origin. For example, Nietzsche believed that the idea of human equality was bred of the resentment of the weak at the power their strong and dominant masters had over them in ancient warrior societies. So what if it was the resentment of slaves against their masters that was the origin of belief in human equality, Rorty countered. Human freedom and equality are good ideas no matter their origin. You don't discriminate against a good idea because of its origins. You classify ideas according to their relative utility rather than by their sources.[18]

By that standard, religion has been the source of a number of values that continue to be useful to society, even if we reject religion's account of their origins. Trying to love your neighbour as yourself is an admirable thing to do, even if you do not believe it was originally commanded by God, because you cannot believe God was ever there to command it.

The pragmatic approach to religious faith will never persuade unbelievers to believe, but it may persuade them to respect and value those who do, because of the good that can result. It takes us back to Macaulay's common frontier between opposing beliefs, the place where opponents try to listen to each other, and where they have to learn to look both ways. A friend describes this position as 'liminal poise',[19] but in my experience, it can be an uncomfortable place to find yourself. Always easier to have both feet planted on the same side than one here and one there. Safer too. If you stick firmly to one side of a divide, you'll have the support and approval of those behind or beside you. Find yourself straddling a frontier, and you are mistrusted by both sides.

So why don't I commit myself wholeheartedly to one side or the other? Because I feel the attraction of both sides but cannot settle confidently in either place. I have felt the pull of transcendent meaning. I have experienced the joy of union with everything that is. I have taken part in the dance of life's meaning. But I have also looked into the abyss, have experienced the contradiction, the impossibility of finding meaning in a world so soaked in pain. I am writing this on the seventy-fifth anniversary of the liberation of Auschwitz. What meaning am I supposed to find in that? Adorno said there could be no poetry after the Holocaust, the Shoah. A more important question is whether or how religion can continue to have any meaning after it and all the other horrors of history. And it brings me back to where I started this journey: with Joan's problem, the problem of suffering.

PART IV

SUFFERING: WHY IT'S A PROBLEM FOR SOME BUT NOT FOR OTHERS

VIII

JOAN'S PROBLEM

I began this book with the problem of suffering and I want to return to it now and take the discussion forward, because, after the existence of the universe itself, suffering is the greatest problem that confronts the religious consciousness – by which I mean the sort of mind that can't help asking if there is any meaning in or beyond the universe. For the person who believes there is no ultimate meaning because there is no ultimate meaner, the *problem* of suffering does not arise. In a meaningless universe with no purpose other than its own blunt existence the question of suffering does not arise as *a question*. In such a universe, anything can happen, and why not? None of it means anything.

Mind you, those who believe there is no meaning to the universe are not thereby spared suffering – no one is – but for them it is not a *moral* problem, only an unpleasant fact. But for those who believe or want to believe that the universe has some sort of purpose, the fact of suffering, especially unrequited suffering, creates a number of intolerable difficulties. Some types of religious consciousness reject any attempt at justification or explanation. For them, not even the existence of an allegedly good God with a

149

plan to make it all better at the end of the story can justify what goes on while it is spinning. Their revulsion is absolute, especially when it is confronted by attempts to offer what appear to be excuses for or explanations of the divine intention or purpose in a world so saturated in pain. The greatest fictional exemplar of this refusal to enter the conversation or play the justification game was Dostoevsky's Ivan Karamazov, whom I quoted in the prologue. Let me remind the reader of his words:

> I want to be there when everyone suddenly finds out what it was all for. All religions in the world are based on this desire, and I am a believer. But then there are the children, and what am I going to do with them? That is the question I cannot resolve . . . there are hosts of questions, but I've taken only the children, because here what I say is irrefutably clear . . . if everyone must suffer, in order to buy eternal harmony with their suffering, pray tell me what children have to do with it? It's quite incomprehensible why they should have to suffer, and why they should buy harmony with their suffering . . . It's not that I don't accept God, Alyosha. I just most respectfully return him the ticket.[1]

For Ivan, it was the suffering of children that took him out of the God game, but even a cursory glance at the evidence will show us how *universal* suffering is. And it is not confined to the human animal. On a news programme the other night I caught a glimpse of the eyes of a beast in a crowded truckload of cattle being exported for slaughter. It knew, somehow, what was happening to it.

Maybe not as absolutely as the Jews who were stuffed onto the death trains to Auschwitz understood what was happening to them, but *somehow*. Animals can sense their death, smell it, know it's coming. You can see it in their eyes as they are caught by the throat in the teeth of a superior predator. There is even a terrible beauty in it, a symmetry of horror, as one creature preys upon another in the dynamic food chain of animal life.

Charles Darwin saw little beauty in it. In a letter he sent to his friend Hooker in 1856, Darwin wrote: 'What a book a Devil's Chaplain might write on the clumsy, wasteful, blundering low and horridly cruel works of nature.' And in a letter to Asa Gray four years later in 1860, he made the point specific: 'I cannot persuade myself that a benef-icent and omnipotent God would have designedly created the Ichneumonidae with the express intention of their feeding within the living body of caterpillars.' The hideous thing about the Ichneumonidae is that they sting their prey not to kill but to paralyse, so their larvae can feed on fresh, live meat.

Caterpillars aside, in the animal kingdom there is usually life *before* death for most creatures in the wild. But not once we humans invade their lives. One of the most poignant aspects of our industrialised food industry is the occasional glimpse the television camera affords us of what goes on behind the scenes, like the mournful gaze of that beast in the cattle truck I saw a few days ago. But that is far from the worst. Every year, a few weeks before Christmas, the great turkey holocaust gears itself up for slaughter. It is only rarely that we get a look into one of those enormous windowless sheds where thousands of turkeys are crammed together and deprived of anything remotely like a life before they are killed to satisfy our craving for cheap food. No daylight or fresh air. Everywhere the hum of ventilators and the noise of as many as 20,000 turkeys, shuffling from foot to foot, pecking at dry pellets in the automatic feeders, sipping water from the drinking bells, each confined to an area the size of the roasting tin that will be its final destination. Built into the economics of the industry is the concept of the 'starve out': hundreds of thousands of birds who can't make it to the feeders or drinking bells and are left there to die of starvation or thirst. The most surreal aspect of these massive death camps is the masturbation shed, where the turkey stags are held in vices while being masturbated every few days. Their semen is then milked into a tube and injected into the female. The stags are huge, unwieldy birds, with bald patches on their wings and feathers where they have been repeatedly held in the masturbation vice. When they attempt to move, they wobble painfully and laboriously. These are creatures who have never had a *life* in any meaningful sense of the word. Technically they are *alive*, but only just. They are *product*, their status as living creatures an awkward but necessary interlude in their painful journey to the shelves of our local supermarket.

Grim establishments like this are dotted all over the British countryside. I see one regularly from the window of the train that commutes between Edinburgh and Glasgow, and I wonder at the misery it represents, the thoughtless cruelty it proclaims. Long rows of windowless wooden sheds with the look of places that have something to hide. What is hidden is the industrialised torment of tens of thousands of birds before they are slaughtered for our consumption. No longer is there any sense that they belong to nature and deserve a life, however brutish or short it might be. The intensive, industrialised farming of poultry is humanity's own version of the Ichneumonidae wasp.

But it is not only turkeys and chickens we have slaughtered industrially. We've done it to each other with equal callousness in the wars and purges that are a constant feature of our history, not to mention the genocides and organised persecutions orchestrated by all those ruthless optimists with their perfect plans for our salvation. The number for these slaughtered in the twentieth century alone is beyond computing: thirty-seven million killed in the First World War; sixteen million killed in the Second World War; six million Jews gassed by Hitler in his concentration camps, not to mention all the other undesirable types he got rid of in his campaign of racial cleansing. (Incidentally, the concentration camp system was copied from the camps established by the British in South Africa during the Boer War at the turn of the twentieth century). Anything between three and five million Russian peasants killed by Stalin in his collectivisation experiments in the 1930s, not to mention the thousands he purged for the wrong political opinions. And as many as forty-five million killed by famine in China during Mao's Great Leap Forward in the 1950s. As well as the pain we have inflicted on each other in our addiction to warfare, there is the arbitrary suffering of good people leading their ordinary lives, often in the service of others.

It is these startling contrasts that have led some of our

best moralists to argue not *against* God, as Ivan Karamazov did, but *for* God and a life beyond this one where these wrongs could be finally righted and these sufferings compensated. The angle here is not the justification of *God* for having come up with such a rotten system – the argument Ivan Karamazov rejected – but the longing good people have to see wrongs righted and innocent people compensated, the very basis of every civilised legal system in human history. This is why some of our noblest thinkers have felt *obliged* to hope for another life. Not for their own sake, not because they selfishly wanted their own lives to go on for ever, but in order to squeeze some moral sense out of the universe and even out its colossal injustices. This is how the philosopher Mark Johnston expressed this position:

> Faced with the professional torturer who dies calmly in his sleep at a ripe old age surrounded by his adoring family, and the nurse who, for her whole life, cared for the dying only to herself die young and alone from a horribly painful and degrading illness, people tend to fall into despair over the importance of ethical goodness. Unless, that is, they have hope or faith.[2]

Commenting on this passage in his review of Johnston's book, *Saving God*, the philosopher Galen Strawson offered this reflection:

> It makes the heart sink most strangely to consider that those who do nothing but good in life experience nothing but intolerable suffering – to the point that

they are unable to have any sense of their value – and are then extinguished for eternity. This sinking feeling can seem like a proof: a proof that the importance of goodness is, as Johnston says, at risk from the insult of unmitigated death. Certainly, many people who want there to be an afterlife care more about the idea that it will allow for justice to be done than they do for their own personal survival. Others simply want there to be a space where those who have suffered intolerably can know something else, and this is all too understandable.[3]

'. . . *many people who want there to be an afterlife care more about the idea that it will allow for justice to be done than they do for their own personal survival*'. These are generous and important words in thinking about the problem of suffering. Strawson is not a believer, either in God or in life after death, but he recognises here that the religious temperament at its best is seeking not its own survival or glorification, but an answer to an intolerable problem – the unrequited suffering of good and innocent people.

These were not the people Ivan Karamazov had in mind in his great rejection of God. His eyes were on the great explainers who set out to clear God of any blame for the suffering that characterises his creation. They are practitioners of an ancient theological art called 'theodicy' – from the Greek words for God and justice – the technical term used to label the department of religion that attempts to answer or justify the problem suffering poses for believers in God *for God's sake*, rather than for the sufferer's sake. Think of an advocate in court trying to prove the innocence of the accused he is defending, though here it is God who is in the dock. Theodicies come in many shapes and forms and some of them are found in the sacred scriptures of particular faith communities. One of the most dramatic is found in the Hebrew Bible, where it is set forth in one text and challenged in another, an example of the Jewish genius for *arguing* about God, rather than slavishly following official theories about him.

In the Hebrew tradition the earliest theory – *theory* is probably too thought out a word here, and *instinct* may be better – is a kind of moral catch 22. If you are suffering it is evidence that you have sinned and are being punished, because the good do not suffer, only the wicked. Therefore, the question to ask the suffering is, *what have you been up to?* Here's Psalm 37:

> I have been young, and now am old;
> yet I have not seen the righteous forsaken
> or his children begging bread.

> The righteous shall be preserved for ever,
> but the children of the wicked shall be cut off.

Not only does God actively reward the righteous with prosperity, he actively *punishes* the wicked with adversity. If you are having a hard time, if you have lost everything, then God must be punishing you for your misdeeds, however secret and hidden they may have been to others. Ugly it may be, but it's a theory that's had a long shelf life and can be heard today in the cry of the suffering, 'What have I done to deserve this?' And it operates at the

group as well as the personal level. God is not only understood to punish individuals for their misdeeds; he punishes
whole societies for the misdeeds of their members. We
heard this line from Christian fundamentalists in the US
after 9/11, which some of them interpreted as God's
punishment for the vices of liberal Americans. A similar
accusation was made by Muslim clerics in Indonesia after
the tsunami on Boxing Day 2004. God was cleansing the
land of the corrupting effects of Western tourism on their
previously pure Islamic society.

The great thing about the Hebrew tradition is its
capacity for arguing with itself. Remember: two Jews, three
opinions. In what Christians patronisingly call the Old
Testament there's a whole book that challenges the
received view, the Book of Job. It does not solve the
problem of suffering for believers in a good God or offer
an alternative theory. What it does is dispute the claim
that it is God's punishment for sin. It shows us a righteous
man overwhelmed by suffering not because he has done
anything wrong, but because God has taken a bet on him
with Satan that no matter what they throw at him he will
not, as Satan suggests to God, 'curse thee to thy face'.
God plans a test to prove whether Job's piety is sincere
or just a prudent calculation to guarantee his continued
prosperity. Even at this stage in the tale a subtle under-
mining of the official theory is going on: we are told that
Job is undoubtedly righteous, so his prosperity could be
said to lend support to the traditional view; but we also
know that, for no reason other than his own whimsical
interest in the test, God is about to deprive Job of the
official rewards of genuine virtue. The first five verses

establish both Job's immense wealth and his genuine piety. Then it continues:

> . . . there was a day when his sons and daughters were eating and drinking wine in their eldest brother's house; and there came a messenger to Job, and said . . . 'the Sabe'ans fell upon them and took them, and slew the servants with the edge of the sword; and I alone am escaped to tell you.'
>
> While he was yet speaking, there came another, and said, 'The fire of God fell from heaven and burned up the sheep and the servants, and consumed them' . . . there came another, and said, 'The Chalde'ans formed three companies, and made a raid upon the camels and took them, and slew the servants with the edge of the sword' . . . there came another, and said, 'Your sons and daughters were eating and drinking wine in their eldest brother's house; and behold, a great wind came across the wilderness, and struck the four corners of the house, and it fell upon the young people, and they are dead . . .'
>
> Then Job arose, and rent his robe, and shaved his head, and fell upon the ground, and worshipped. And he said, 'Naked I came from my mother's womb. And naked shall I return; the Lord gave, and the Lord has taken away; blessed be the name of the Lord.' In all this Job did not sin or charge God with wrong.[4]

Job knows that whatever is happening to him can't be a theological *quid pro quo* or tit for tat, because there was no *pro* to justify this *quid*. The heart of the book is a series of encounters between Job and three old pals, all fervent exponents of the official theory that suffering is evidence of guilt. They come to get Job to fess up and admit he has been up to something, which can be the only possible explanation for his condition. Baffled and angry, Job refuses to yield. He has done nothing to deserve the tragedies that have overwhelmed him. But how can you prove *what you haven't done*? If the evidence is never discovered that will vindicate him in this life, he trusts that after his death God will be his advocate and disprove the charges:

> . . . I know that my vindicator lives and that he will rise last to speak in court . . . my defending counsel, even God himself.[5]

Job does not have to wait for death to get his vindication. God denounces Job's accusers 'for not having spoken of me what is right' and Job is rewarded with 'twice the possessions he had before'.

It has to be admitted that if we want answers to the problem of suffering, then reading the book of Job will be a disappointment. What it does is destroy the power of what may be the oldest effect suffering can have on the afflicted, which is to give them a sense of their own complicity in what is happening to them. They feel that, somehow, they have brought it on themselves. And there are always people around who will support this kind of self-sabotage. When a friend of mine was dying of cancer, she was visited by someone who patted her hand, smiled pityingly and said, 'Who hasn't been looking after herself?' She replied, 'Do you think telling me, however nicely, that

I am responsible for the lymphoma I have, is helpful to me?"[6]

Cancer apart, the afflicted often do feel they are somehow responsible for what has befallen them. In spite of the Book of Job, the idea persisted in the Hebrew tradition that they had brought their age-long sorrows upon themselves. It dies hard this idea. Even where we think there may be elements of truth in the diagnosis – such as diseases related to lifestyle – it still leaves unanswered the question why the universe is organised in such a way that it allows us to develop habits that can kill us. *Unanswered* for the religious imagination that is, the type of imagination that seeks for meaning and casts around itself for *explanations*. More of which are to follow in the Christian and Islamic traditions where the tone was always more assertive and declaratory than in the Hebrew tradition of struggle and questioning.

In both Christianity and Islam there is an explanation that is the obverse of the absolute atheist position – that what happens just happens because that's the way things are in a universe with no moral purpose or meaning. No point in getting upset. The script's already been written or is being improvised by factors beyond our control. The difference between the secular and religious versions of this kind of fatalism is that the theologians who posit it attribute it not to ontological roulette, but to God. It's called 'predestinationism' and there's a brutal logic to it. God created the world and everything in it. God is all-powerful and all-knowing, so everything that happens is according to his guiding will. It is all there already in the mind of God, predestined, scripted, plotted down to the tiniest gesture. Here's how the Protestant theologian John Calvin put it, and note how he historicises the Adam and Eve myth in his first statement of the doctrine in a way already familiar to us from our earlier examination of the Garden of Eden myth:

> All of us, therefore, descending from an impure seed, come into the world tainted with the contagion of sin. Nay, before we behold the light of the sun we are in God's sight defiled and polluted. 'Who can bring a clean thing out of an unclean? Not one,' says the Book of Job. We thus see that the impurity of parents is transmitted to their children, so that all, without exception, are originally depraved. The commencement of this depravity will not be found until we ascend to the first parent of all as the fountain head. We must, therefore, hold it for certain, that, in regard to human nature, Adam was not merely a progenitor, but, as it were, a root, and that, accordingly, by his corruption, the whole human race was deservedly vitiated.[7]

After the Adam and Eve myth, the other root of Calvin's theory probably lies in some obscure words by Paul the Apostle in his Letter to the Romans:

> . . . we know that in everything God works together for good with those who love him, who are called according to his purpose. For those whom he foreknew he also predestined to be conformed to the image of his Son, in order that he might be the first-born among many brethren. And those whom he predestined he

also called; and those whom he called he also justified; and those whom he justified he also glorified.[8]

Not easy to figure out exactly what Paul was getting at here, but Calvin was in no doubt. He wove the story of the Fall of Adam and Eve into Paul's predestination theme and came up with his own version of the doctrine, whose logic went like this: because we all inherit Adam's guilt and 'come into the world tainted with sin' we deserve and are destined for eternal damnation. But for reasons known only to himself, God decides to save some from hell, while the rest get what they deserve.

By predestination we mean the eternal decree of God, by which he determined with himself whatever he wished to happen with regard to every man. All are not created on equal terms, but some are pre-ordained to eternal life, others to eternal damnation; and, accordingly, as each has been created for one or other of these ends, we say that he has been predestinated to life or death. We say . . . that God by his eternal and immutable counsel determined once for all those whom it was his pleasure one day to admit to salvation, and those whom, on the other hand, it was his pleasure to doom to destruction.[9]

Though there is no funny side to this grim doctrine, one of Scotland's greatest writers saw macabre possibilities in it. In James Hogg's *The Private Memoirs and Confessions of a Justified Sinner*, the *justified* sinner – that is one who has received assurance from God that he is among the elect

162

predestined for salvation – is Robert Colwan. Colwan decides that since sinners are already on their way to hell, he'll speed them along by getting rid of them early, so he embarks on a career as a serial killer.[10]

We find the Colwan mind-set in Islamic suicide-bombers, whose self-destruction at the press of a button has the desirable double effect of propelling them into paradise and their infidel victims into hell. Which is apt, because we find a version of the doctrine of predestination in the Qur'an, where Suras 9 and 36 suggest that everything that happens to us has been scripted by God. Even though the Prophet has been sent to humanity with the final revelation, there are some whose necks are in fetters because they are predestined to reject the truth of his message.

> Naught shall visit us but what God has prescribed for us . . . The Word has been realized against most of them, yet they do not believe . . . We have put on their necks fetters up to the chin . . . and We have put up before them a barrier and behind them a barrier; and We have covered them so they do not see.

It is spelled out even more explicitly in one of the *hadiths*:

> There is no one of you, no soul that has been born, but has his place in Paradise or in Hell already decreed for him, or to put it otherwise, his unhappy or his happy fate has been decreed for him.[11]

You don't have to be a Calvinist or a follower of the Prophet to buy some version of this account of the vagaries and tragedies of human behaviour, this sense that our ticket's already been stamped, even if it is only for the postcode lottery that determines where we'll be born and what our social circumstances will be. On the flip side of the religious predestination coin, some secular determinists take a not dissimilar line. They argue that our behaviour in any given situation is a consequence of how and what we came to be. Our nature and character, formed by genetic and circumstantial factors that were never in our control, determine our actions. The cosmic roulette wheel spins and our little lives find their pre-ordained slots and the game goes on. And we are not *ultimately* responsible for any of it. To be *ultimately* responsible for our actions we would have had to have been ultimately responsible for the factors that prompted them, that ancient sequence of linked events going all the way back to the Big Bang. In fact, if we could have traced every tremor and surge of this multiplicitous sequence of cause and effect we could probably have predicted all the outcomes that flowed from the originating explosion. Not because some omniscient author intentionally plotted every event and consequence in our lives, but because of the impersonal nature of the innumerable contingencies that prompted every choice made in human history. If everything were known and if we lived in laboratory conditions where the contingencies and chance happenings in every life could be kept on record from the moment of anyone's birth, then their choices might appear foregone conclusions. But we do not live in such conditions, so we can never know all that happened in the past to influence us and inform our choices. We feel free because we act against a background of ignorance. We are like amnesiacs who do not know who they are or where they came from. That's why Spinoza said that what we think of as our freedom is actually a form of ignorance. We can never know all the facts and contingencies that determined the choices we made in life. At the granular level our lives seem to operate a bit like Heisenberg's Uncertainty Principle, which famously stated that we cannot measure precisely and at the same time the position and the velocity of an object – even in theory. At the subatomic level there are things in nature we cannot predict because they do not follow the law of cause and effect, which would suggest, however hard it is to comprehend, that there can be effects without causes, things that just happen. And back we go to that originating singularity and our search for what 'caused' *it*. If the universe itself can be thought of as a causeless effect, where does that leave our search for meaning and purpose in our own lives?

Whether we like it or not, uncertainty seems to be ingrained in the nature of the universe, and it is why we can never predict the impact on a human life of events at its earliest or subatomic level. Another reason why we should be slow to judge the actions or motives of others. Who knows what factors went in to making them what they became? And yet . . .

Why does something about this reasoning sit uneasily with us? Why is that we can agree with the logic behind it, yet continue to feel responsible for our actions and their effects on others? Though we might admit that much of our behaviour is determined by factors beyond our control or understanding, nevertheless the practice of self-examination and the self-knowledge it can help us acquire promise a level of self-transcendence that can weaken and even divert the unpredictable drives of our nature. It can give us enough leverage to modify our character and turn it in a different direction. Religious history is full of individuals who claim to have been 'born again' because they submitted themselves to energies that countered the drive and direction of their given nature. William James used the phrase 'twice-born' to characterise them. The phrase suggests that what we were given to be at birth, the role predestined for us, may yet be improvised in a different direction. Nor is religion the only stimulus to this kind of rebirth. Counselling and psychoanalysis can have the same effect, as they encourage us to explore our own history and identify the facts and forces that formed us. Understanding ourselves better, we can write a different script for ourselves. We do not have to accept that our lives have been propelled by indeterminate forces beyond our control. We can choose to become agents of our own destiny.

This suggests the possibility of something else as well, something about the universe. If there is something in *us* that allows us to transcend the millennial forces of our own nature and character – an opening towards *self-direction* or agency – might not the same be true of the universe as a whole? Might it not have a capacity for self-transcendence or even *self-expression*? Might there be the possibility that the universe is more *active* than we imagine and that it may even be capable of *making itself known to us*? That it may have a type of agency we find it hard to credit it with?

This came home to me in a conversation I had with the

nature writer Richard Mabey. We are used to the idea that the other animals we share the planet with have little or no agency in their lives, no capacity for creativity. Like animated machines, they are programmed by nature to do what they do. Unlike us, they are not *self*-conscious, have no understanding of themselves as individuals. Which is why we find it easy to slaughter them, often for the fun of it. Richard Mabey did not argue in *theory* against that view. He gave me an example that contradicted it. He had heard birds improvising in their singing – in effect, doing jazz. Jazz happens when musicians respond to each other and make unscripted music never heard before. Mabey had heard birds doing that. They weren't just feathered robots programmed to pour out their songs. They were capable of making new music in response to other birds. They did jazz. They had *agency*.

Is it not possible that the earth itself is a living entity capable of agency, which is why our brutal exploitation of its resources is another example of our capacity for genocide? It's a stretch, but is it not possible to see some level of agency and creativity in the evolution of species through natural selection? Nature making itself up as it went along, improvising on its own trumpet? And may not our attitude to these ideas call us to the liminal poise that renders us incapable of jumping to absolute conclusions about any of this – because it is able to look both ways? It also takes us back to the pragmatic test of our beliefs. What are the consequences of holding them? One consequence of recognising the earth as possessing a living identity would be to afford it the same reverence and care we bring – in theory at least – to our treatment of our fellow human beings. Whimsical or not, it might have prevented us exploiting it in a way that may render it uninhabitable in the foreseeable future.

The idea of the world possessing agency and the capacity for self-disclosure intrigued our brilliant old friend Martin Heidegger. Heidegger wondered if the failure to accord the possibility of an active as opposed to a passive presence to the world – what he called our 'forgetfulness of Being' – was the reason we had replaced reverence for the creation with an instrumental attitude towards it that has allowed us to exploit it for selfish gain. Not unlike the way women feel men objectify their bodies and lose sight of the person or presence that inhabits the object of their desire. This forgetfulness of the being of women closes men against their *active presence*. No longer subjects that reveal themselves, women are reduced to objects for male exploitation. Is this what we are doing not only to the lives of others, but to the world, to Being itself?

This is not a provable argument, of course. Nor an explanation. But, to quote William James again, it should be enough to 'forbid a premature closing of our accounts with reality'. For those of us well used to living with uncertainty, it is reason enough to keep the possibility of the self-disclosing nature of the universe open. But not as a holding operation. Nor as a temporary stop gap till a resolution is incontrovertibly achieved, a state of *pending* till *we know for sure*. We should have the courage and determination to maintain a state of *resolute irresolution*, because that is all our situation honestly allows us. Just because passionate believers and equally passionate disbelievers have closed their accounts with reality – because they *know* the absolute truth about the nature and direction of the universe – is no reason for the rest of us to cave in and apply for a visa to their certainties. If the liminal borderland is where we are most comfortable, if there is no road for us that is right entirely, then let us stay where we are and keep on looking both ways.

IX

MORE REASONS RELIGION
MAKES JOAN'S PROBLEM
WORSE

To switch angles for a moment: wherever religion turns in its attempts to explain how God could have created a universe so soaked in pain, it hits *moral* difficulties.

Pause... I've just written that sentence twice. Or edited it. First, I had written: 'wherever religion turns in its attempts to explain how a *good* God could have created a universe so soaked in pain...' But the adjective stuck in my throat and I spat it out. Maybe I should have written 'religion's God' rather than a 'good God', because it should be obvious after reading the preceding chapter that the God of religion can be a cruel monster with nothing good about him. That's certainly true of the God of predestination. In the secular obverse of the doctrine, determinism, at least there is no one to blame. It's just the way the Great Universal Machine operates. It spews us all out regardless, some to sorrow, some to joy. But the 'God' of predestination knows what he's doing and does it because he can, like any other bored psychopath seeking diversion. There are softer theodicies, some of which I'll look at in this chapter, but they all fall under a similar condemnation.

Whatever justification they propose, the suffering in the world is always disproportionate to the *religious* explanation offered.

Which is why we have to think a bit more about the 'God' of religion as opposed to the 'true' or 'real' God, who may or may not exist, and who is beyond all our attempts to define and describe – maybe even to know. One way to start thinking about this is to return to those mystics who angered ecclesiastical authority by claiming that *all* human talk about God was, by definition, idolatrous. Since no human language could express or encompass the mystery of God, anything we said about the divine mystery was us talking about ourselves and projecting it onto a blank screen and calling it 'God', a 'God' always and inevitably made in our own image. It is no surprise, therefore, that the excuses we make on 'God's' behalf for permitting or even *promoting* suffering all reflect human thinking and theorising. Worse: they reflect all the human vices, especially cruelty. Nowhere is this clearer than when we start thinking about the role of *punishment* in human history, an enthusiastic theme in certain branches of Christian theodicy, though its exponents like to disguise it in softer words such as *chastisement* or *discipline*.

I am writing this a few days after the Scottish government banned the smacking of children, even by their parents in the privacy of their own homes. A few years ago, corporal punishment was finally banned in schools. These moves represent a significant shift in human thinking about the value of violence in the rearing and training of children. When I was a child, corporal punishment was a standard element in all Scottish schools. The pain-deliverer was a long, split leather strap called a 'tawse', applied ferociously to the open hands and wrists of children by their teachers for a variety of misbehaviours. I was a turbulent child, so I was belted regularly in both primary and secondary school. The headmaster of my primary school was known as Tawser Murray because he was such an enthusiastic practitioner of the craft. It was the done thing at the time, and by the standards of the punishments of the past it was relatively benign, but the tawse hurt and could leave a child's hands red and raw for days. This latest reform represents the shuddering finale to a truly grim history in which the infliction of pain on children was justified in the name of a moral theory, though it was always also about something darker – *the pleasure it gave to the punishers*.

That's why Nietzsche, possibly borrowing the words from Goethe, warned us to 'Beware of all those in whom the urge to punish is strong'. A warning the human community has paid little attention to, until very recently. Think of the punishments we've doled out in the past, some of them still practised in certain cultures today. Floggings. Whippings. Executions. Crucifixions. Beheadings. And they were (are) always guaranteed to draw an enthusiastic crowd. What's behind it all? Oh, there was always a bit of justificatory theorising attached to it – which I'll come back to in a minute – but most of what was going on was sadism, *pleasure in inflicting pain on others or in watching it being inflicted*. Nietzsche got the diagnosis right:

It was here . . . that the uncanny intertwining of the ideas 'guilt and suffering' was first effected – and by now they may well be inseparable. To ask it again: to what extent can suffering balance debts or guilt? To the extent that to make suffer was in the highest degree pleasurable, to the extent that the injured party exchanged for the loss he had sustained, including the displeasure caused by the loss, an extraordinary counterbalancing pleasure: that of making suffer – a genuine festival . . . To see others suffer does one good, to make others suffer even more: this is a hard saying but an ancient mighty, human, all-too-human principle . . . Without cruelty there is no festival: thus the longest and most ancient part of human history teaches – and in punishment there is so much that is festive.[1]

Public executions in Europe used to be festivals that attracted large crowds, just as they still do in Saudi Arabia today. Michel Foucault described one that happened in 1757. Damian, a soldier who had tried to assassinate Louis XV, was condemned 'to make the amende honorable before the main door of the Church of Paris'. This involved having the flesh from his breasts, arms, thighs and calves torn away with red hot pincers and the wounds that resulted filled with molten lead, boiling oil, burning resin, wax and sulphur. His body was then pulled apart by four horses – *drawn and quartered* was the technical description. Damian remained alive and aware during this whole process. Finally, what was left of him was burned to ashes and the ashes thrown to the winds.[2] Special seats for wealthy Parisians were provided for this festival of punishment, because: '*Without cruelty there is no festival: thus the longest and most ancient part of human history teaches – and in punishment there is so much that is festive.'*

When these festivals of punishment were banned in Europe, the gratification they promised did not cease; it shifted behind the grey walls of schools, reformatories and orphanages. We know from countless memoirs and news stories, not to mention the harrowing testimony in recent child-abuse cases, that gross physical punishment was a conspicuous feature of many Christian schools and care establishments. We know now that it gave the floggers and beaters sexual gratification – *without cruelty there is no festival* – but we also know there was an ancient theory behind it that justified it *theologically*.

My hunch is that the *theory* probably came first – *punishment is good for the soul* – and the gratification it brought to those who delivered it was an incidental benefit discovered later. The inflictors realised that as well as doing their duty by inflicting pain, they were also beginning to enjoy it, so it became a self-fulfilling feedback loop of gratification. It does not matter whether the theory came first or whether, as Nietzsche suggests, gratification was always the primary motive. The fact is that punishment became a big trope in the thinking of the theologians of theodicy, though it was never entirely clear whether God only permitted others to inflict it for our ultimate good or whether God actively *inflicted* it as well – also for our salvation.

Forget Calvin and the Qur'an for a moment. It's God the Punisher we are thinking about here, not God the Exterminator. We'll have to look at the Bible again, as well as at some later theories, to figure out whether it is one or both. But to repeat the question, does God only *permit* punishment? Or does God, so to speak, enjoy a bit of the action himself? There are passages in both the Hebrew and the Christian scriptures that suggests that it is the latter: God actively punishes us for our own good. Here's a verse from the Book of Proverbs in the Hebrew Bible:

> My son, do not despise the chastening of the Lord; neither be weary of his correction: For whom the Lord loveth he correcteth; even as a father the son in whom he delighteth.[3]

That would suggest that God is an *active* punisher. Or is that a matter of interpretation? Are we to understand here that we are to take the suffering that comes upon us *as if it came from God*, and in that way make something out of it, turn it to a good use? That is the sense these words from Proverbs are given when they are quoted in a New Testament text of unknown authorship, falsely attributed to Saint Paul, known as 'The Epistle to the Hebrews'. The title of the letter – *to the Hebrews* – is significant. It was written for Christian *Jews*, as all the first Christians were, who were tempted to give up on the infant Church because they were being given a hard time by their fellow Jews for claiming that Jesus was the long-expected Messiah, especially since his imminently predicted return to complete the transformative work he had started was being indefinitely delayed. The author of Hebrews wanted them to endure the pains they were suffering and remain true to Christ. He exhorted them to endure the punishment *as if it came directly from God.*

175

In your struggle against sin you have not yet resisted to the point of shedding your blood. And have you forgotten the exhortation which addresses you as sons?

'My son, do not regard lightly the discipline of the Lord, nor lose courage when you are punished by him. For the Lord disciplines him whom he loves, and chastises every son whom he receives.'

It is for discipline that you have to endure. God is treating you as sons: for what son is there whom his father does not discipline?[4]

Both Proverbs and Hebrews reflect a world in which harsh physical punishment or the *disciplining* of children and wrong-doers was the norm. We get that, know the history. We've only just given it up ourselves. But it still does not add up to any kind of *explanation* as to why God – if there is a God – came up with a world in which cruelty and suffering are such marked features. It is one thing to acknowledge that enduring suffering can be character-building for us. It can build our courage. And it can help us to identify with and work to alleviate the sufferings of others. This is what motivates former addicts to help their fellows get clean. It is why women who've been in abusive relationships with men run shelters other women can escape to once they've plucked up the courage to leave. History is full of these compassionate reversals. But none of it comes close to justifying God's role in the system, if it is a *system*. Are we to believe that God intentionally contrived a scheme of such torment in order to provoke our compassion and ability to endure? The Bible comes close to saying that, but never quite gets there. Boiled down by interpretation, it tells us what we already know: suffering is horrible and there is too much of it, but enduring it can deepen us and teach us compassion.

But some of the stories told by later theologians to explain why there is so much suffering in the world definitely suggested that, at least as a theoretical possibility, it was in God's mind from the beginning. They point out that it would have been easy for God to create a world without suffering, full of perfect, happy creatures, like cows contentedly munching the grass in meadows that never withered or failed. But they would have been automata, machines that did what they were programmed to do. *They would have been incapable of loving the God who made them, freely, of their own choosing.* And, we are told, that is the kind of love God longs for.

Pause here for another moment, please. Interesting idea that, God's longing for love. It suggests incompleteness. Makes God like you and me. Needy. And back we come again to the mystics who tell us *all* our God-talk is us-talk, is us talking to ourselves about ourselves. But how could it be anything else? Who else is there to talk to or to talk about? It reminds us yet again that theology, in spite of the inordinate claims it makes for itself, is a human art, which is why it has been said that 'God' is the strongest character in world fiction.[5] *Or maybe, just maybe, something more?* Something that leaves open the possibility of revelations. But back to the theologians' story.

They tell us that since God wants our love not our bovine contentment, he takes a momentous risk. He creates the world as a Vale of Soul-Making in which we are free not only to love and care for each other, but to come to know and love God as well. In order to achieve this, God has to place us at a certain distance from him, much the way we might watch our children through a one-way window to see how they are behaving, without their knowing we are watching them. They don't *know* we are there. Nor can we absolutely know that God is there. That's the arrangement between us and God. And that's why there has to be the *possibility* of suffering in such a world, the result of the free choices we have made. That's why there is so much wrong-doing and misery on earth. *It is a necessary consequence of our freedom to choose right or wrong.*[6]

The glaring omission in this theory is suffering in the animal kingdom, not to mention the pain caused by natural disasters. All that stalking and hunting and killing. That vivid fear in the eyes of stricken animals. Those devastating earthquakes and tsunamis. Not to mention the diseases and injuries that can afflict any of earth's creatures. I suspect that the reason for the omission of animals in Christian theodicy was that they were not reckoned to have immortal souls, so they were not included in the salvation plan. God had not created animals in order to win their love and call them back to him for ever. He had created them for the exclusive use of humans. They were human food – *turkeys*. Remember?

Be fruitful, and multiply, and fill the earth and subdue it; and have dominion over the fish of the sea and over the birds of the air, and over every living thing that moves upon the earth.[7]

Another awkward element in the soul-making theory is the massive assumption it makes about the freedom of the human will. It suggests that we all arrive in the Vale of Soul-Making free of any social or genetic context, pure and unconnected to the past. No *previous*, as the police would say. Immaculate. A blank sheet. Now we know that is far from the case. We have already thought about the fact that we arrive loaded with a lot of material that pre-determines the kind of life we'll lead. It may be an inherited disease or condition. It may be an inherited disposition or defect, some kind of neurological deficit or flaw in our immune system that we'll pass on to our children, sometimes with devastating consequences. Even if we insist on clinging to some version of freedom of the will, it is obvious that it has been modified by factors inherited and circumstantial that were never under our control.

Nevertheless, the suffering of animals, the pitiless impact of natural disasters and its question-begging assumptions about human freedom aside, there is a kind of beauty in the Vale of Soul-Making theory, and not a little truth. Love is not love that is compelled, not freely given. And if there is that supreme mystery we call 'God', it certainly seems to keep what one theologian called an '*epistemic distance*' between us, 'epistemic' from the Greek for knowledge.[8] An important aspect of human anguish is that we don't and can't *know* for sure if God is there or not, which is why we argue endlessly about God's existence and nothing ever seems to clinch the debate once and for all.

Yet from somewhere there comes to some of us a sense of a presence waiting to be discovered or acknowledged *though it will not force itself upon us.*

Is there some huge attention, do you think,
Which suffers us and is inviolate,
To which all hearts are open, which remarks
The sparrow's weighty fall, and overhears
In the worst rancour a deflected sweetness?
I should be glad to know it.[9]

That's the bit of the soul-making theory that can touch us. The idea of a broken-hearted God who loves us, waiting with immemorial patience for us to turn aside and *see*. We have rehearsed that scenario often enough in our own human affairs. The quiet, faithful, patient loves we spurned for the sake of their glamorous rivals. The impatience that prevented us from making those slow discoveries that required patience and the capacity to sit still. Is it *there*, that infinitely patient waiting love? Maybe not. *Probably* not. But isn't it strange that this great blasting brute of a universe has produced creatures with such unappeasable longings for it?

Perhaps all our loves are merely hints and symbols; vagabond language scrawled on gate-posts and paving-stones along the weary road others have tramped before us; perhaps you and I are types and this sadness which sometimes falls between us springs from disappointment in our search, each straining through and beyond the other, snatching a glimpse now and then of the shadow which turns the corner always a pace or two ahead of us.[10]

For some it is more than *hints and symbols* and *vagabond language*. There are those who have been convinced not by

180

the teasing *absence* of God, but by an overwhelming sense of God's presence. They tell us that 'God' is not an idea contained in a form of words but a way of being towards others and towards Being itself. Reverent. Expectant. Wordless. Never controlling, because love and goodness *cannot be compelled.* We should do good for its own sake *as if God did not exist.*

The phrase in italics at the end of that paragraph – *as if God did not exist* – is a translation of a famous Latin phrase with an interesting history: *etsi deus non daretur.* Its first use comes in the work of Hugo Grotius (1583–1645) a Dutch lawyer and theologian, who used it in his study of *On the Law of War and Peace*, where he argued that we should establish our principles of justice on our natural instinct for what is right and good *as if God did not exist.* Though Grotius did not take his own insight as far as this, its effect is to warn us against allowing organised religion to dictate our morality. Good should be done for its own sake and not because it is commanded by some version of religion's God, especially since we know how often in the past religion's God has been used for evil purposes. Better to do the right thing *as if God did not exist* than to do the wrong thing in the name of God *whose existence you are certain of.* It turns out that our greatest danger is not living *without* God. It is to mistake our own projections *for* God, and come up with a god in our own image, packed with our own hates and insecurities – an *idol*, a human construct. Better no-God, *a-theos*, than that false God.

The theologian who carried this disturbing insight in the most intriguing direction was the anti-Nazi martyr, Dietrich Bonhoeffer. Arrested for his part in a plot against

Hitler and hanged on 9 April 1945, while on death row Bonhoeffer wrote a number of remarkable letters to his friend Eberhard Bethge on developments in his theological thinking. In one written on 16 July 1944, he applied Grotius's term to religion.

> God as a working hypothesis in morals, politics, or science, has been surmounted and abolished, and the same thing has happened in philosophy and religion. For the sake of intellectual honesty, that working hypothesis should be dropped, or as far as possible eliminated . . . And we cannot be honest unless we recognize that we have to live in the world *etsi deus non daretur*. And this is just what we do recognize – before God! God himself compels us to recognize it. So our coming of age leads us to a true recognition of our situation before God. God would have us know that we must live as men who manage our lives without Him. The God who is with us is the God who forsakes us . . . The God who lets us live in the world without the working hypothesis of God is the God before whom we stand continually. Before God and with God we live without God.[11]

There is a lot to think about in that difficult passage. His fundamental idea is that men and women *have come of age*. Which brings to mind the status and limits of childhood. Children are protected and taken care of till they grow up and come of age, when they start taking responsibility for themselves. But there is loss in becoming an adult. Loss of the rapture of magical thinking. Loss of fairyland. Loss of Santa Claus. Bonhoeffer is suggesting a parallel between our ancestors and our own childhood. He says that, compared to us, our ancestors were children when it came to their understanding of 'morals, politics, and science'.

Reflecting on science is the best place to explore what he meant. Back then when we were childish in our knowledge, we believed God had made the world in six days, six thousand years ago, and that on the sixth day he brought humans forth, as fully formed then as they are today. We now know that was magical thinking, childish thinking. Science tells us how unimaginably slow the process was, and that there might not even have been any creative agency behind it. The emergence of the universe might have been an effect without a cause, as Heisenberg's Uncertainty Principle provokingly suggests.

And the same uncertainty applies to the story of our moral evolution. Back then we believed that one afternoon on a mountain top in Sinai, God carved the moral law for us on tablets of stone, for ever. Now we know what a long and fitful struggle the genealogy of our morality has been over the centuries, and how it keeps shifting in our own day, often by defying these old God-given prohibitions.

Bonhoeffer is telling us what we all know in our hearts, if we'll admit it to ourselves: these old myths were the stories we were told in our childhood. Now that we have come of age, we should put them aside and take responsibility for ourselves like adults, even if some of us long for the days when religious authorities told us what to do and what to think. Bonhoeffer had anticipated this turn in his thinking in an earlier letter written a few months before on 30 April:

You would be surprised . . . by my theological thoughts
and the conclusions they lead to . . . What keeps both-
ering (or gnawing at me) incessantly is the question
what Christianity really is, or indeed who is Christ really,
for us today? . . . We are moving towards a completely
religionless time; people as they are now simply cannot
be religious anymore.[12]

These letters have prompted reflection in many people
who find themselves attracted to Christ but repelled by
religion. Is it possible, they ask themselves, to follow Christ
etsi deus non daretur? To have Christ without God? Or
without certainty about God? Those were the questions
Bonhoeffer asked himself on death row. One of the things
he meant by *religionless Christianity* was the absolute imperative of opposing evil and injustice for its own sake, even
if there is no God. Of doing good for its own sake, not
because God commands it. The paradox is that Bonhoeffer
believed that's what God wanted as well. God wanted us
to live and act righteously *as if there were no God.*

What this means is that faith in the *true* God is action
not belief, a verb not a noun. Something *done* not an idea
held in the mind. The test always lies in the consequence
of the belief. How does it prompt us to act towards others?
If it encourages us to evil, according to Bonhoeffer, then
it is not belief in the true God; it is just another projection
or version of the self that wants to submit itself to the
dictation of an absolute power, in order to avoid the pain
of critical thinking and moral uncertainty. Something in
us longs to be told what to do and what to think by a
power beyond ourselves. And the authority or god we

submit ourselves to can even be a defiantly godless one that asserts its godlike power over us by denying the existence of all other gods. There was a lot of that godless absolutism in the twentieth century, all those ruthless optimisms that were prepared to wipe out whole populations in pursuit of their perfect plans – and succeeded only in increasing the size of the already depthless ocean of human misery.

We need to stretch our understanding of religion to include any absolute ideology – godly or godless – whose authority over us forces us to diminish or afflict the lives of others. That's what Bonhoeffer meant when he said that if we are to do Christianity today, we must do it *without religion*. Good must be done for its own sake, even if it means opposing what religion calls 'God'. It must be done even if we believe that the universe is indifferent to our struggles and is uninterested in our values. It must be done even if we decide there is no solution to Joan's problem, the problem of suffering, because there is no god to solve it. There may be no solution, but there can be a response. We can choose to bind up wounds, not inflict them. We can choose to withstand the afflicters, whatever the cost. And in every generation, there are always some who do. That's why reading history can be a tonic as well as a depressant. It reminds us that as well as persecutors there have always been comforters. As well as tyrants, there have always been those who withstood them, even unto death. And isn't it intriguing that such a universe has produced creatures who would rather die than conform themselves to its glacial indifference to suffering? Isn't it strange that in such a universe pity weeps over the world's sorrows and tries to bind up its wounds? This is not an *argument* of course. No *therefore* follows. Only a doubt, a wondering, a pause at another frontier.

As we pause, we should reflect on the fact that, as well as encouraging us to evil deeds in the name of its god, religion can encourage us to hold evil *theories* as well. And nowhere is this clearer than in the conflicting ways Christianity has interpreted the death of Christ. Let me remind you of the question from Nietzsche I quoted at the beginning of this chapter.

> To ask it again: to what extent can suffering balance debts or guilt? To the extent that to make suffer was in the highest degree pleasurable, to the extent that the injured party exchanged for the loss he had sustained, including the displeasure caused by the loss, an extraordinary counterbalancing pleasure: that of making suffer . . .

If we can remove the idea of pleasure from those words and concentrate instead on the idea of suffering as a way of balancing debts or guilt, then one branch of Christian theodicy suggests that God insists on suffering to *atone* for sin. The religious word 'atonement' carries an interesting meaning for some of us today. In modern theories of what is called 'restorative justice' the victims of crime are brought together with their offenders in order to repair a rupture or heal a wound. The victim expresses the shock and devaluation that the offence caused. The sense of outrage and disorientation. The destruction of order and meaning. *This is what you did to me. You shattered my world, broke my life in pieces.* And it gives the offender the opportunity not only to hear about the impact of the offence on the victim, but the chance to own and repent of it. In this way what had been broken is brought together again, or *'At-Oned'*, as some theologians gloss the idea of atoning. These same principles are applied to Christian atonement theology, but with an intriguing twist. One idea is that the sins knowingly committed by us in the Vale of Soul-Making accrued a debt of guilt that had to be satisfied. But who was to pay it? And to whom?

An intriguing aspect of Christian atonement theology is that it was never formally defined into a compulsory doctrine, like the Doctrine of the Trinity. Remember the Athanasian Creed that warned those who didn't believe it that *without doubt they would perish everlastingly*? Well, the Church never got around to applying the same deadly rigour to belief in the atonement, which probably accounts for the different ways theologians have tried to explain it. Here are a few of them. It is worth noting how they reflect the culture of their time and place, another example of how theology, whatever ecclesiastical authority says, is always *human thinking transcendentalised.*

The earliest go at atonement theology was what theologians call the 'ransom theory', probably provoked by a verse in Mark's Gospel where Jesus describes himself as giving his life *as a ransom for many.*[13] We know what ransoming is. It goes on today when a greedy or aggrieved group of some description kidnaps travellers and demands a ransom for their return. In the case of Jesus Christ, we have to ask who the capturer is to whom the ransom has to be paid. In early atonement theory the terrorist in

question was the Devil, which is why it is an uncomfortable theory for modern theologians to accept, since many
of them no longer believe in the Devil. The Church's
earliest theologians had no problem with the Devil. To
them, in the words of The First Letter of Peter, he was
a roaring lion who walked about 'seeking whom he may
devour'.[14]

Sometimes the account offered was straightforward. The
Devil was the Lord of Evil, so when humans sinned, they
put themselves under his control and had to be bought
back or ransomed. Or it could be thought of as defaulting
on mortgage payments and having your house repossessed.
A stretch, I know, but theology loves these metaphors and
analogies. Here's another even more colourful and
far-fetched one. The Devil was a predator fish like a shark,
hunting and swallowing sardines/sinners. But Jesus was
not a sardine/sinner. Jesus was sinless, so when the Devil
tried to swallow him, he got stuck in the Devil's throat.
Jesus was bait to land the shark. Colourful though it is,
you won't hear that version of atonement theology today,
unlike the next one, which is very popular in evangelical
circles.

It's called the 'satisfaction theory', and it was developed
in the high Middle Ages when the idea of *honour* was a
fundamental value in courtly society. In medieval thinking
the weight of an offence was increased the higher the
status of the person against whom it had been committed.
And only a person of equal or higher rank could atone
for the wrong done. Offend a peasant, no problem, easily
dealt with. Offend a baron, more difficult, but do-able.
Dishonour the monarch, you're in real trouble, unless you

can borrow a king from somewhere. Offend God? You are absolutely done for. Because God's dignity is infinite and human sinners are finite, there is no mortal of sufficient rank to pay off the debt or restore the honour that was lost. By the measure of the theory of honour, only God could pay it off himself. But it isn't God who owes it, so who is to pay it off, and to whom? That's the human predicament. Only someone both human and divine could pay off the debt. So out of the depthless kindness of God's heart, in the person of Jesus, God assumes human nature and offers himself to himself to atone for the guilt incurred against himself. In the crucifixion of Jesus, the God/Man satisfies the divine debt.

Later versions of the satisfaction theory took it in a darker direction. They saw it not as a debt another might assume, the way I might, as a friend, offer to pay off your hire-purchase arrears. The shift was to see the debt due not as cash but as *retribution – punishment*. I might agree to pay off your loan but can I take your punishment for you if you'd been sentenced to a flogging – or a crucifixion? A different deal entirely. Here we have shifted from the idea of *debt* to the idea of *guilt*. A guilt that has to be *punished*.

Here we should recall all those floggings and chastisements that characterised early human approaches to guilt, most of which we've long-since abandoned. Not here. Not with what is called the 'penal satisfaction theory'. It is not only ugly, its ethics and legality are dodgy. Some human transactions *are* negotiable. As a friend, I can pay off your debt. The company you owe the money to isn't bothered about *who* pays. All it wants is its money back. Money, debts of that sort, *can* be transferred. But can guilt for a crime? If I kill someone and am found guilty and sentenced to life imprisonment, would any judge allow my guilt to be transferred to a friend to do time for me, supposing I could find one to volunteer? Maybe we could see a way in which such a substitution might be possible in some circumstances. That is what the Dominican priest, Maximilian Kolbe did in Auschwitz in 1941. He substituted himself for another prisoner and died in his stead. But pause for a moment and ask this question. Who was Father Kolbe satisfying here? The Nazis. The Third Reich. *Evil.* Who was the crucified Christ satisfying by *his* death? I guess it has to be God. God the Nazi? Well, what word would you use to describe a god who insisted that someone had to die to satisfy his outraged honour?

It dies hard, this old idea that God relishes punishment. And it takes us back to the fact that all our God theories are projections of our own cultures and their compulsions and cruelties. They are all *our* stories, endlessly told to help us figure out where we've got to in the haunted wood. That's why they are all so obviously related to the times and cultures that prompted them. That was how they tried to figure it out back then in those circumstances, entangled in those cultural imperatives. But, in Bonhoeffer's phrase, we have now come of age. Which is why so many elements of those cultures revolt us today, as do the stories they told to try to explain themselves to themselves. That's always how it plays as we wander through the trees.

Doesn't this cursory sketch of atonement theory under-line yet again the obvious fact that religion and the theology it composes are creative arts, and not *science*, as its proponents try to claim? It's all *stories*, things we tell each other in our attempts to make sense of our lives. Some of the stories are cruel and ugly *because so are we*. Some of them are kind and loving *because so are we*. More reasons for taking them seriously, but never *literally*. Whether they like it or not, even the most conservative believers are selective in the choices they make from the library of stories in their own traditions. I know preachers who insist on proclaiming the death of Jesus as the punishment God demanded of sinful humanity. I don't know any who interpret Christ as fish bait to hook the Devil. But both are in the collection. It just depends which one you take down from the shelf.

However, there is one story that came out of all this ponderous theologising that can touch our hearts even if it does not persuade our reasons. It is the claim not that God demands suffering from us to appease *his* honour but that, like a heart-broken lover, God pays all our debts because he feels all *our* sorrows. It is the idea that when *we* suffer, God suffers in, through and with us. It is called the 'exemplarist or example theory'. Easy to explain and understand. The death of Jesus is a shining example of love to us. *He loves us enough to die for us!* And it inspires us to follow his example and try ourselves to live lives of sacrificial love. As an *explanation*, it doesn't work any better than any of the others, but there is something about it that can move to tears those who meditate on it. To be unconditionally loved can be transformative. To be loved like that can break your heart and change your life. But there's no point in getting forensic or *scientific* about any of this. It's another story. And because theology is a *creative art* – though theologians rarely make good artists – I'll go to an artist to see it expressed.

The exemplarist theory is associated with the great medieval theologian Peter Abelard, famous for his love-affair with Héloïse, a love for which he was gelded by her outraged relatives, condemned by the Church as a heretic, and sent into exile. His story is beautifully told in Helen Waddell's novel *Peter Abelard*, published in 1933, the year Hitler became chancellor of Germany. In the novel she reimagines the sorrows of their affair and how its aftermath influenced Abelard's theology. In the passage in the novel where the exemplarist idea hits him for the first time, Peter is in retreat in the country with his friend and supporter, a young priest called Thibault. It is All Saints' Day, and they are preparing to celebrate the festival in the little thatched oratory they've built. Peter has returned from a melancholy walk and Thibault is unpacking their provisions.

'My God,' said Thibault, 'what's that?'

From somewhere near them in the woods a cry had risen, a thin cry, of such intolerable anguish that Abelard turned dizzy on his feet, and caught at the wall.

'It's a child's voice,' he said. 'O God, are they at a child?'

'A rabbit,' said Thibault. He listened. 'There's nothing worrying it. It'll be in a trap. Hugh told me he was putting them down. Christ!' The scream came yet again.

They plunge down to the river bank and find the rabbit jammed in a trap.

The rabbit stopped shrieking when they stooped over it, either from exhaustion, or in some extremity of fear. Thibault held the teeth of the trap apart, and Abelard gathered up the little creature in his hands. It lay for a moment breathing quickly, then in some blind recognition of the kindness that had met it at the last, the small head thrust and nestled against his arm, and died.

It was that last confiding trust that broke Abelard's heart. He looked down at the little draggled body, his mouth shaking. 'Thibault,' he said, 'do you think there is a God at all? Whatever has come to me, I earned it. But what did this one do?'

Thibault nodded. 'I know,' he said. 'Only – I think God is in it too.'

Abelard looked up sharply.

'In it? Do you mean that it makes Him suffer, the way it does us?'

Again Thibault nodded.

'Then why doesn't He stop it?'

'All this,' he stroked the limp body, 'is because of us. But all the time God suffers. More than we do.'

Abelard looked at him, perplexed. 'Thibault, do you mean Calvary?'

Thibault shook his head. 'That was only a piece of it – the piece that we saw – in time. Like that.' He pointed to a fallen tree beside them, sawn through the middle. 'That dark ring there, it goes up and down the whole length of the tree. But you only see it where it is cut across. That is what Christ's life was; the bit of God that we saw. And we think God is like that, because Christ was like that, kind, and forgiving sins and healing people. We think God is like that for ever, because it happened once, with Christ. But not the pain. Not the agony at the last. We think that stopped.'

'Then, Thibault,' he said slowly, 'you think that all this,' he looked down at the little quiet body in his arms, 'all the pain of the world was Christ's cross?'

'God's cross,' said Thibault, 'And it goes on.'

'The Patripassian heresy,' muttered Abelard mechanically. 'But, O God, if it were true. Thibault, it must be. At least, there is something at the back of it that is true. And if we could find it – it would bring back the whole world.'[15]

The Patripassian heresy? Think first about the word *heresy* there. Another one of those ideas we are told we must not even consider. Another concept we should never allow to enter our brain. Banned. Forbidden, *on pain of* . . . You know the score by now. You've encountered it in all those *gnosticisms*, all those systems of perfect knowledge and their festivals of cruelty for those *who do not believe* . . . But if you are interested in the big word, it simply means 'Father-suffering', a God who bears our sorrows and feels our pains.

What's interesting here is that while it was denounced as a heresy by the early Church, it made a comeback after the Holocaust and the other horrors of the twentieth century, when some theologians began talking about the crucified God, the suffering God. But it leaves us with a question. What if the God we think we have been encountering or responding to is just ourselves *deified*? What then? We know we are capable of great evil, so should it be any

surprise that we find that version of God – that version
of ourselves – in the stories composed by the artists whose
work was collected into what later readers called the Book
and we call the Bible? All that divine rage and the slaughter
it provoked. All that smashing of heads against the stone.
All those knives flashing above ordered sacrifices. *Us deified.*
God fashioned in our image. Absolutising and anointing
our darkness.

But we are also capable of heroic kindness and sacrificial love, so God comes in that image too. Some of the
tenderest stories we have ever told ourselves have been
about the God who comes to us on wounded feet,
imploring us to love one another as he loves us. 'Like as
a father pitieth his own children,' so is God overflowing
with love towards us, we are told.[16] *Us again.* God fashioned
in the image of our own capacity for mercy and loving
kindness.

Which of these stories do we choose to live by? Or to
put it another way: which version of God are we choosing?
A further question follows. With God or without God, what
is the effect, what is the consequence for others, of the
story we have chosen to follow? Cruelty or kindness? Hatred
or love? Contempt or understanding? What Bonhoeffer
wanted us to get here was that love is its own meaning. It
does not have to be the effect of a preceding cause, such
as a divine prompting. It does not require any external
justification. To adapt Heisenberg, it can be understood as
pure uncaused effect. It *is.* And because it is, the lives of
others can be made better. Love done not because it is
commanded by transcendental authority, but because it
is the right thing to do – even if no transcendental authority

exists. Better: *because* no transcendental authority exists. It doesn't matter which, as long as the good, the kind thing is done. And in his prison cell, facing death, that's what Bonhoeffer came to think the God he continued to believe in wanted too.

Before God and with God to live without God!

That means to follow the way of love for its own sake, *as if there were no God.*

Again, no justifying argument offered here. No explanation. Just an acknowledgement of the strange fact that this great bruising thrust of nothingness, this pitiless exploding singularity, tells itself stories through us that challenge its own vast indifference.

Looking up at the stars, I know quite well
That, for all they care, I can go to hell,
But on earth indifference is the least
We have to dread from man or beast.

How should we like it were stars to burn
With a passion for us we could not return?
If equal affection cannot be,
Let the more loving one be me.[17]

Pause. What have I learned from this journey through the stories we have told ourselves about the universe and our place within it? A few useful things. That cogent stories can be in conflict with each other and that we should be in less of a rush to give one or other the victory. This is not the same thing as declaring a draw. It is not that neither has won, but that both may have won, both may be true, because reality is stranger and sometimes more beautiful than we can comprehend. That is why, even if it is not a posture that appeals to us personally, we should allow others the right to maintain themselves in a state of liminal poise, of looking both ways. With God and without God.

But a more important conclusion is that for us the big question is no longer how we came to *be*, but how we *are*, how we choose to live. How we act. What does it profit us if we resolve all the questions the existence of the universe poses for us, and destroy ourselves in the process? Because it is now more obvious than ever that we ourselves are the biggest problem we face. We have spent much of our history destroying each other. Now we are well on the way to destroying the earth itself. The urgent task is to find a story that will help us face down our own compulsive destructiveness and save ourselves and the world. Several good ones are on offer. What follows is the one I try to live by.

X

THE STORY I TELL MYSELF

B ut to repeat: I am not trying to persuade the reader into or out of any particular way of understanding the world. One way or another, we are all trying to figure it out. It's just that I want to resist those who claim to have it figured out exactly and perfectly, and are out to compel the rest of us to see it the way they do. This passion to persuade is normally associated with the sales departments of religious and political systems. How could it not be? If you are persuaded that you are in on the secret, you'll obviously want to share it. And part of the secret is always the command to spread it, the compulsion to persuade others. To *save* them. It may just be standing at a street corner on a Saturday morning pushing a newspaper that contains the good news of the coming political kingdom. Or it may be buttonholing strangers and getting them to listen to your urgent message, warning them of the danger they are in, unless they repent and believe.

Aren't we all doing it, one way or another? Selling our story? And much of it is attractive, even moving. Persuading your friends, *you must see this* or *you must read that* or *you must meet so-and-so*. There's now a whole industrial complex dedicated to this activity of selling our ideas or marketing our brands. Every organisation or institution with any sort of ambition now has a Communications or 'Comms' department dedicated to the task of selling or promoting its unique selling points or 'USPs'. We are all compulsive storytellers. Explainers. Marketeers. Evangelists. But I want to make a distinction between the stories we try to sell to others and the stories we honestly try to live by ourselves. I don't think this is just exhaustion or persuasion-fatigue after a life spent wrestling with religious meaning, though there may be some of that in it. It might even be a kind of despair. But it is hard to avoid despair in the face of the crimes and follies and tragedies of human history.

I write this on a day when I read in my newspaper about how the world's super-rich are expected to buy 8,000 new private jets over the next decade, the largest and longest-range version of which will contain 'four true living spaces, including a full-size kitchen and a master suite containing a full-size bed'. That story was juxtaposed with developments in the story of the thirty-nine Vietnamese migrants – smuggled into Britain by people-traffickers – who were found dead in a refrigerated trailer in Essex. I've spent a lot of time in this book looking at the way religion has tried to explain or justify these and other hideous contrasts. I called it 'Joan's problem', because Joan Didion wrote about it so plangently. Only a problem, of course, if, like me, you suffer from the compulsion to search for meaning in what may be a meaningless universe, indifferent to all our sorrows.

I have already suggested that while there is obviously no answer, no theoretical solution, to the problem of suffering, there can be a response. And we all make it, one way or another, whether or not we acknowledge it. It brings me back to what I think is the fundamental question life presents us with. Given that the universe is what it is – however you understand it – what are you going to do about it? How have you personally decided to respond? What story have you decided to live by? Whether or not you know it, you are already living by a story you are telling yourself. So, what difference does your story make? Upon whom does it impact? Are you aware of its impact? Come to think of it, do you even know the story you are living by?

Here's the story I have chosen. One way or another I've been trying to live by it all my life, but now I understand it differently, tell it differently. The difference is that I no longer have any interest in understanding it or justifying it theoretically or theologically. I am only interested in its practical import. Only in what it prompts me to do. And what it prompts me to stand against. It is the story of a first-century Jew called Jesus. His story has been described as the greatest story ever told, maybe because it gathers together many of the themes that have obsessed the human imagination for centuries. In his magnificent new study of the Bible, this is how John Barton describes it:

> King's College, Cambridge, holds a 'Ceremony of Nine Lessons and Carols' every Christmas Eve, broadcast throughout the English-speaking world and imitated in many churches . . . As the title indicates, it includes nine readings from the Bible, interspersed with hymns and carols . . . The Bible is seen here as telling a story of disobedience and redemption, of sin and salvation, of

paradise lost and paradise regained, concerning the whole human race . . . The Bible is thus understood as a story about a disaster followed by a rescue mission, and this fits with the nature of Christianity as a religion of salvation.[1]

Stories about disasters followed by rescue missions are as old as storytelling itself. They come from a deep need in our psyche, the place that loves stories of deliverance and rescue, because we often feel ourselves to be the captives of forces we resent and long to be liberated from. In a previous chapter I touched on Nietzsche's theory of the genealogy of morals. He thought that many of the values we rate highly today had their roots in the resentment of the weak against the strong. Equality and human rights may be important values *now*, but they had their origin in the hatred of weak or enslaved people for the magnificently strong warriors who dominated them. Nietzsche called the values provoked by this resentment of the strong by the weak 'slave morality'. What he admired was the courage of those with strong enough characters to make their own values and stamp their personal impress upon history. The fact is that some of our most important moral discoveries may have had resentful origins, but that does not diminish their significance and usefulness today.

We find a similar dynamic at work in some of religion's deepest themes. To understand the Jesus story and answer Bonhoeffer's question about what it might mean for us today, we have to perform a similar exercise in social and political archaeology. It takes us back to the Roman Empire in the first century CE, a perfect example of the kind of warrior society Nietzsche admired for its ruthless self-confidence. In a speech the Roman historian Tacitus put into the mouth of the Caledonian general Calgacus, who was resisting the Roman invasion of Scotland sometime around 84 CE, the Romans are described as '. . . robbers of the world . . . To plunder, butcher, steal, these things they misname empire: they make a desolation and they call it peace'. The Romans did not prevail in Caledonia, but on the other side of the world in Palestine they absolutely succeeded in plundering and making a desolation. And one of their victims was a Jew called Jesus from Nazareth in the tetrarchy of Galilee. To the Romans he was just another nuisance they despatched with their usual ruthless efficiency, except that this one became a story that is still being told. What do we know about him? Not a lot, but enough. In the earliest writing about him, Mark's Gospel, he walks into history without prologue or explanation:

. . . in those days Jesus came from Nazareth of Galilee . . .[2]

We know a lot about the social and political stage onto which he strode, probably around 30 CE in Palestine, a troublesome but unimportant outpost of the Roman Empire. The American sociologist the late Gerhard Lenski, divided human societies by technology and ecology into hunting and gathering, horticultural and industrial societies. By this definition, the Roman Empire was an agrarian society that forged iron ploughs, harnessed animals for traction, and used wheel and sail to move goods. More significantly, it was characterised by an impassable gulf between the upper and lower classes. At the top of the pyramid were the ruler and governors, who made up 1 per cent of the population but owned half the land. On the side of the rulers there were three other classes: priests, who could own as much as 15 per cent of the land; retainers, ranging from military generals to bureaucrats; and the merchants, who could end up with considerable wealth and some political power. Almost at the bottom of the pyramid were the peasants, the majority of the population, about two thirds of whose annual crop went to support the upper classes. Below them were the artisans, dispossessed members of the peasant class who had become a wandering workforce. And right at the bottom were the degraded and expendable classes, about 10 per cent of the population.

Where did Jesus fit into this finely layered stratification? Mark tells us that he belonged to the artisan class. The context in which he gives us this information is significant. We hear it in an incredulous aside, one of those 'Who does he think he is?' questions the gifted often provoke in their neighbours. Jesus had started teaching, and his hearers were both amazed and offended by his eloquence.

> . . . many who heard him were astonished, saying, 'Where did this man get all this? What is the wisdom given to him? What mighty works are wrought by his hands! Is not this the *tekton*, the son of Mary and brother of James and Joses and of Judas and Simon, and are not his sisters here with us?' And they took offense at him.[3]

They were outraged because Jesus was only a '*tekton*', someone who worked in the building trade, misleadingly translated 'carpenter' in most versions of the New Testament. During the lifetime of Jesus, a few miles away from Nazareth there was a building boom at Sepphoris, under the direction of the local client king or tetrarch of Galilee, Herod Antipas. There were few trees in Galilee but there was a lot of stone, which was probably why Jesus used metaphors from stonemasonry in his teaching but said little about joinery. We can't be sure about any of this, of course, but it seems likely that Jesus, far from serving his time in a cosy village carpenter's workshop, spent most of his life labouring on a large building site in a busy and expanding city. According to the New Testament scholar John Dominic Crossan, that placed him in 'the dangerous space between Peasants and Expendables'.[4] He belonged to and spoke on behalf of the poor who struggled each day for their daily bread. Most of what we know about him comes from the last few years of his life, the preaching years that ended in his crucifixion.

Is there anything else we can discover about him from what are called 'the hidden years' before the start of his public ministry? Guess-work mainly, derived from what social anthropology can tell us about the life of people of his type and class at that time and place. Would he have been able to read? According to the gospels the answer is yes, but Crossan is not so sure. He tells us that 95 to 97 per cent of the Jewish state were illiterate at the time. Not that illiteracy is a bar to eloquence, especially in an oral culture used to handing on its traditions through memorisation. The Scottish writer James Kelman described the eloquence of unlettered people with a gift for language as 'orature', the capacity to compel and persuade through the spoken word alone. Whether or not he could actually read them, Jesus certainly knew and wielded to great effect the stories his people had told about themselves, as well as the longings and questions the stories always prompted. The most insistent questions they asked were the ones asked by defeated people everywhere: '*Why?*' and '*When?*' Why all this suffering, and when will it end? Questions with a particular poignance for the Jewish people. The stories they had learned from their own history told them they were a chosen people, elected by God for a special purpose. But all that seemed to be special about them was their suffering, a suffering that intensified under the iron rule of the Romans.

Not that there was anything new in that. For hundreds of years their homeland had been plundered by outsiders. The cast list of what Tacitus would have called their desolators might have varied over the centuries, but the effect was always the same. More than five hundred years before the time of Jesus, the Assyrians had conquered them and taken thousands of them into exile in Babylon, an exile from which some of them were allowed to return in 538 BCE. After the Assyrians it was the Greeks. In 333 BCE, the Greek emperor Alexander the Great was the chief desolator of the day, but at least he hadn't tried to interfere with their *religion*. He had allowed them to follow their own traditions. The trouble started when he died and his toleration policy died with him. The king who opened the next chapter of their suffering was Antiochus IV. Greek by descent and disappointed in his ambition to be a major player in the region, Antiochus took his anger out on these stiff-necked Jews who refused to compromise their religious convictions. In 167 BCE he turned the temple in Jerusalem into a shrine to the Greek god Zeus and sent enforcers throughout the land to compel the Jews to make sacrifices to him.

During the revolt that followed, another story was composed by an unknown writer. Written in code, it was intended to strengthen and comfort the Jews during yet another period of persecution. But it wasn't just meant to comfort them. It was also intended to answer the 'when' question, the question oppressed people always ask their gods: when are you going to intervene and save your people? And it introduces us to a new type of story called 'apocalyptic', from a Greek word meaning to uncover or unveil what was previously hidden, the way a theatre curtain is pulled back to reveal the action on the stage. Another way to think of an apocalyptic writer is as an intelligence agent in on God's plan for the final and triumphant fight-back against the occupying enemy. Apocalyptic is another kind of *gnosis*, another version of the secret knowledge that will transform history. It lets us in on the future. Like a movie trailer, it announces and gives us a preview of what's coming next.

The most significant apocalyptic storyteller in the Hebrew Bible is one of its latest entrants. He called himself Daniel, and he put his message into a short text only his Jewish readers would have been able to understand, albeit with a bit of headscratching as they tried to puzzle it out. It was written in response to what Antiochus was doing in Jerusalem in 137 BCE, but its setting was Babylon during the time of the exile, more than three hundred years before. Like other apocalyptic texts – Revelation, the last book in the New Testament, is another example of the genre – it was dense with weird dreams and strange stories. The most famous story featured Daniel, a Jew exiled in Babylon during the Captivity who had become an official of the Persian Empire. We are told that Daniel was greatly admired by King Darius not only for his competence as an administrator, but for his fidelity to his god. Daniel's eminence attracted the jealousy of other officials and they set a trap for him. They persuaded Darius to impose a law decreeing that throughout the empire for *one month* no one would be allowed to pray to any god *other than Darius himself*. Anyone who broke the law was to be thrown into a den of lions. Darius duly passed the law, but regretted it when he was told that Daniel continued to pray to his own god during the month prescribed for monarch worship. But having signed the law he saw no way out of his dilemma, so Daniel was sent into the den of lions – from which he emerged unscathed the following morning.

Daniel's listeners would have known his story was not about what had happened three hundred years ago in Babylon. It was about what was happening in Israel now, during their persecution by Antiochus. It was telling them that though they had been cast into the den of lions, if they stood fast God would save them. But strengthening their resistance wasn't the book's only purpose. Daniel believed he had been shown the future, the future he longed for, the kind of future oppressed people always pine for. It promised him that *God's agent of salvation was coming soon to rescue them*. The One to Come would end history and its sorrows, and inaugurate a universal kingdom of justice and peace.

> I saw in the night visions, and behold, with the clouds of heaven there came one like a son of man, and he came to the Ancient of Days and was presented before him. And to him was given dominion and glory and kingdom, that all peoples, nations, and languages should serve him; his dominion is an everlasting dominion, which shall not pass away, and his kingdom one that shall not be destroyed.[5]

Whatever Daniel thought he was doing, his story expressed one of the unappeasable longings of the human imagination: the idea of a perfected society in which the world's lost innocence will be restored and the Golden Age before the Fall will return. In this story there is always a Fall into suffering that needs to be consoled, and a ruined Eden that needs to be restored. Apocalypse is the dream of the wretched of the earth at all times and in all places for the 'beautiful return', the 'grand instauration'.

A heartbreaking example of another plundered and desolated people with an apocalyptic dream is the story of the horseriding tribes of Native Americans who had lived freely for centuries on the Great Plains, before the United States government herded them into reservations in the nineteenth century. The Great Plains covered an area well over a million square miles, stretching from Canada in the north to Mexico in the south. It had been roamed by herds of buffalo that supplied almost all the needs of the tribes who had shared the vast space with them. Into that Eden came wave after wave of white settlers, pursuing their own dream of a Promised Land somewhere at the end of the Western Trail. The buffalo were hunted to extinction, partly as a policy to starve the Native Americans into retreat, and partly for the pleasure of slaughtering wild game that some humans become so strangely addicted to. Defeated and desolated, the original inhabitants of the land were resettled in reservations and their long sorrow began.

But in 1889 a Paiute mystic called Wovoka had a vision like Daniel's. He saw all Native Americans taken into the sky. Then the earth opened and swallowed all the white people. And their old life on the plains was restored to what it had been before their Eden was plundered. In his dream Wovoka was told all this would come to pass if his people started dancing. And the apocalyptic movement known as 'ghost dancing' began. Wovoka prophesied to his people that if they danced long and hard enough the wild horses and buffalo would return to the plains to wander again among the whispering grasses. So they started to dance. The movement spread to other tribes. Still Eden did not return. They danced harder. Some of them danced themselves to death. But the earth did not fall upon the white people and bury them. Wild horses did not sweep over the crest of a beloved hill, their manes flashing in the sun. Buffalo did not thunder out of the north calling them again to the thrill and communion of the chase.

What happened was that the U.S. Bureau of Indian Affairs became concerned that so many Native American tribes were gathering together. They feared insurrection, revolution. When the dance spread to the Lakota tribe, the bureau's agents arrested the most respected of the Lakota leaders, Sitting Bull. Sitting Bull's death in December 1890 and the massacre of two hundred Native Americans at Wounded Knee, not the restoration of Eden, was the result of the ghost dancing dream. Apocalyptic movements like the ghost dancers are cries of longing by broken people for an end to their ancient suffering. The fact that the promised end never comes only increases their yearning. Maybe next year.

Nor did the failure of Daniel's dream kill the longing of the Jews for their salvation from their oppressors. The oppression got worse. The persecution under Antiochus was amateur hour compared to what happened when the Romans took over Palestine in 63 BCE and the long endgame began. Continuous unrest followed for 150 years, punctuated by periods of revolt and open warfare. Finally, tired of this people and their inflexible god and the dreams he provoked, the Romans decided to wipe them off the map. After months of hand-to-hand fighting in the streets and alleys of their holy city, the Romans flattened Jerusalem. In the year 70 CE they destroyed the temple. It was over. The long wandering exile of the Jews began.

During these violent final years, two versions of the apocalyptic dream came alive again. One group of dreamers believed the apocalypse would be delivered through a violently enacted revolution, a divinely inspired uprising against the Roman desolators. The Coming One when he finally appeared at the 'end times' would be armed for the 'last battle'. Meanwhile, to destabilise and demoralise the enemy before the 'great coming again', his followers equipped themselves with knives and became experts in wielding them. Like Islamic Jihadists responding to Western interventions in their homelands with knifing attacks on our streets today, the Zealots and Sicarii of the Jewish revolt became experts at slipping their blades between the ribs of Roman soldiers and their collaborators, before disappearing into the night down the alleys and back streets of Jerusalem. It was a guerrilla apocalypse that provoked a ferocious response from the Romans. We know how it ended.

The other group of apocalyptic dreamers believed that when the 'end' came it would be through a transcendental revolution that was the result of divine intervention not of violent human action. The end of history and its sorrows would not be achieved by knife-wielding revolutionaries, but by the mighty arm of God. Apocalypse would be a divine not a human act. All believers could do was look for its coming. They could hold themselves in readiness for its appearing. They could be expectant. They could watch. They could wait eagerly for the curtain to be drawn back and the action to begin. We know how it ended.

Where should we place Jesus in this apocalyptic typology? Though he doesn't seem to fit comfortably into either category, there are elements of both approaches in his teaching and actions. A useful theological term that might help us understand what Jesus was up to is the Greek word *prolepsis*, meaning to throw ahead or anticipate. Political reformers often urge their followers *to be the future you long for and to act as if it were already here.* One way of thinking about the work of Jesus is to see it as the creation of an eschatological community that would live God's end times *now*. He taught his disciples not only to pray that God's kingdom would come on earth as it was in heaven, but to live *as if it were already here*! They were to be a proleptic community. That meant ignoring the barriers and divisions established by the world's religious and political power systems. It identified Jesus not just as someone who waited for God to overturn the system, but as someone who worked to undermine it here and now. Jesus was an apocalyptic revolutionary, a resister. But he was a non-violent resister. His movement did two things. First, it anticipated and exemplified *on earth now* God's kingdom as it would be in all its fullness *then*, when God finally made his move and erupted into history to end time and all its sorrows. Second, in this way and by these means, it sought to get the world *ready* for that coming. The Jesus apocalypse would be in two acts. Act I would be his mission, and its manifesto was contained in the short prayer he taught his followers.

> Our father who art in heaven,
> Hallowed be thy name.
> Thy kingdom come,
> Thy will be done,
> On earth as it is in heaven.
> Give us this day our daily bread,
> And forgive us our debts,
> As we also have forgiven our debtors . . .[6]

Act I ended with the crucifixion. But what about Act II? According to the script Jesus was following, in Act II God would complete the transcendental element of the revolution and finally establish his kingdom on earth as it was in heaven. What happened to it? That depends on how you choose to read the Jesus story.

Like all the other rescue stories we've told ourselves, it takes us back to the sin that got us expelled from Eden and our struggle, ever since, to find our way back. Human history, at both the personal and collective level, can be read through the prism of that foundation story. There's always an original offence that causes an effect that provokes a response that causes another effect that provokes another response, so on and for ever down time's long and winding road. There are feuds and conflicts in the world so long-entrenched that we have forgotten how they originated, and we can never see how they might ever be brought to an end. It is the natural law of offence and retaliation, the oldest, most instinctive, most intractable and most destructive in human history. So entrenched is it in human nature, that our moral and legal reformers only ever sought to order and control it, never to question or replace it. One of the earliest attempts to manage the law of instinctive retaliation is found in the second book in the Hebrew Bible, Exodus, a text Jesus would have known. To avoid the inflation into feud and endless reprisal that our offences can precipitate, Moses established the law of equivalence, of like for like, or tit for tat:

> . . . you shall give life for life, eye for eye, tooth for tooth, hand for hand, foot for foot, burn for burn, wound for wound, stripe for stripe.[7]

But in the non-violent apocalypse of Jesus this way of responding was to be reversed. The law of equivalence was not only to be denied, it was to be transcended.

> You have heard that it was said, 'An eye for an eye and a tooth for a tooth.' But I say to you, Do not resist one who is evil. But if any one strikes you on the right cheek, turn to him the other also; and if anyone would sue you and take your coat, let him have your cloak as well; and if anyone forces you to go one mile, go with him two miles. Give to him who begs from you, and do not refuse him who would borrow from you. You have heard that it was said, 'You shall love your neighbour and hate your enemy.' But I say to you, Love your enemies and pray for those who persecute you, so that you may be sons of your Father who is in heaven . . .'[8]

What forgiveness is intended to do here is to *interrupt* and *redirect* the normal retaliatory impulse that would otherwise add exponential strength to the original offence and push it further into its unstoppable and destructive career. What Jesus proposes is the opposite of what usually happens in human affairs, which is why history goes on repeating itself in both the private and the public realm. The actors may change over the centuries, but the plot is always the same: offence followed by counter-offence; eye for eye; tooth for tooth. Only forgiveness can change that plot. But forgiveness is not a sentimental overlooking of an offending act. Nor is it moral indifference. It is a heroic refusal to let the original offence overwhelm the future, which is what usually happens in our personal and political relationships.

Forgiveness blocks the invasive power of the original offence and stops it spreading further.

In my lifetime I have encountered many examples of forgiveness in personal relationships, but I can think of few attempts to apply its interruptive power to political affairs. An exception was the Truth and Reconciliation Commission in South Africa in 1996. The commission acknowledged what had happened in South Africa during the apartheid years, but it sought to avoid the revenge spiral that might otherwise have followed the ending of white rule, by offering amnesty to those who admitted they had been agents of the apartheid's regime of oppression. Elements of this approach were followed, though less explicitly, in the talks that preceded the Good Friday Agreement in Northern Ireland in 1998. Again, there was an attempt to bring an intractable human conflict to an end by finding a mechanism of agreement that would halt the usual dynamic of revenge and leave the memory of historic offences, however unresolved, parked in the limbo of history.

It would be pushing it to claim that the idea of forgiveness was explicitly present in either of these laudable attempts at peacemaking, but something of its interruptive dynamic was at work. Both attempted to divert historic tragedies into avenues of reconciliation not retaliation. And in their way, each succeeded in redirecting the predestined and destructive flow of history.

Most of us will have experienced the restorative power of forgiveness in our own blundering personal lives, where those who loved us may have refused to accept the severing logic of our behaviour and decided to stick with us. What was revolutionary about Jesus's teaching on forgiveness was how he applied it to the grim political context of his time. It was not heeded then, nor has it been heeded since. But there it is at the heart of his story: a standing challenge to those whose bitterness keeps humanity's religious and political feuds burning and refuses any attempt to extinguish them. Forgiveness is a revolutionary act that can divert and redirect the destructive floods of human history.

The other revolutionary element in the teaching of Jesus was the way he understood the nature of God. Traditional theories were turned upside down. Suffering was no longer evidence of God's disapproval. It was evidence of God's presence. It was where God was to be found, the side God was on. Take all the world's indexes of power and influence. The separation between the rulers and the outcasts. Invert it, turn it upside down or downside up. That's where God would be found. This is what it meant to live God's future now.

> Blessed are the poor *in spirit* . . . Blessed are those who mourn . . . Blessed are the meek . . . Blessed are those who hunger and thirst *for righteousness* . . . Blessed are the merciful . . . Blessed are the pure in heart . . . Blessed are the peacemakers . . . Blessed are those who are persecuted for righteousness' sake . . .[9]

Remember who he was talking about. The people Crossan described as the expendables, those at the bottom of the bottom of the world's pyramids of power.

What are we to make of this? How are we to respond? Are we to depoliticise and spiritualise the radical message of Jesus, the way Matthew tries to do here in the phrases I have italicised, where he suggests that what the poor *in spirit* really hunger and thirst for is not bread and water but *righteousness*? An early example of how the radical message of Jesus has always provoked nervousness in his followers. Crossan won't let them get away with it.

> Did Jesus really think that bums and beggars were actually blessed by God, as if all the destitute were nice people and all the aristocrats correspondingly evil? Is this some sort of romantic delusion about the charms of destitution? If, however, we think not just of personal or individual evil but of social, structural, or systemic injustice – that is, of precisely the imperial situation in which Jesus lived and his fellow peasants found themselves – then the saying becomes literally, terribly, and permanently true. In any situation of oppression, especially in those oblique, indirect, and systemic ones where injustice wears a mask of normalcy or even of necessity, the only ones who are innocent or blessed are those squeezed out deliberately as human junk from the system's own evil operations. A contemporary equivalent: only the homeless are innocent. That is a terrifying aphorism against society because . . . it focuses not just on personal or individual abuse of power but on such abuse in its systemic or structural possibilities – and there, in contrast to the former level, none of our hands are innocent or our consciences particularly clear.[10]

Only the homeless are innocent. What are they innocent of? Complicity in a system loaded against the weak and the vulnerable. Jesus wasn't a philosopher; he was a moral revolutionary, but some philosophers get what he was doing here. An example is the American philosopher, John Rawls. Rawls was interested in what he called 'distributive justice' in society, and the fact that most societies demonstrate the opposite. Distributive *injustice* has been the norm in most societies in history, the Roman Empire being the classic example. In his book *A Theory of Justice*, Rawls suggested that if we wanted to imagine what a more just society might look like, we should first place ourselves in what he called 'an original position' behind a 'veil of ignorance'. 'Original', because the society we are creating hasn't been imagined yet. And 'behind a veil of ignorance', because none of us would know what place we would occupy in the society being planned. If we were in that position of ignorance, we would find ways of helping those who had pulled a weak hand in life – because that might be the situation in which we found ourselves. It's a question of what kind of moral imagination we possess.

Jesus observed how the strong organised the world to suit themselves. And he noticed how their systems and structures generated armies of the hopeless and dispossessed. He warned those in power that when God finally erupted into history at the end, he would boot them off their thrones and replace them with the poor they had stamped on. No wonder he managed to infuriate everyone except the poor who, we are told, *heard him gladly*. He angered those who wanted him to preach violent revolution against the injustices of the system. He angered those who did well out of the system. And he maddened the religious authorities who were complicit in the system, though they appeared to detach themselves from it in order to concentrate on their purity cults and separation strategies and parades of self-righteousness. He described them as 'whitewashed tombs, which outwardly appear beautiful, but within they are full of dead men's bones'.[11] It was only a matter of time before they came for him.

What did the Romans make of him? To them he would have been an unimportant nuisance, and they were ruthlessly efficient at getting rid of nuisances. Their grimmest penalty was crucifixion, grim because it was so *slow*. Crossan tells us that the bodies were left nailed on the crosses till they withered away or were consumed by wild beasts. He writes: 'No wonder we have found only one body from all those crucified around Jerusalem in that single century.'[12] The particular function of crucifixion was to deter resistance or revolt, especially among the lower classes – and the Romans used it liberally. The Jewish historian Josephus tells us that when the Syrian governor Publius Quinctilius Varus arrived in Jerusalem during one of the uprisings, he crucified 2,000 of the rebels.[13] When they eventually came for Jesus, they found him in a garden, another garden. And on the way to the hill of execution they paraded him wearing a makeshift crown of thorns, a cartoon of the domination system he challenged. The Romans loved the joke. He was the joke. The soon-to-be-crucified clown who imagined he could challenge the way the powerful ran the world to suit themselves.

In the face of Rome's calculated ruthlessness, the countercultural strategy of the Jesus apocalypse is heartbreaking in its innocence. To imagine that you could reverse the revenge narrative of human history by the practice of heroic forgiveness. And that you could persuade people to identify not with life's victors but with its victims. Absurd. Not even the Church that claimed to believe his story ever tried to practise it. What it did was preserve it. And keep listening to it – uneasily.

Did Jesus himself really think he could persuade the world to change in this way? Not exactly. As I have already said, he saw himself as the herald or anticipator of a *transcendental* revolution that would be inaugurated by an act of God, when the time came. Till it came, he and his community of rejects and expendables were to be its preview or anticipation. The way they lived was to be the preview or trailer for the Coming Presentation. And as we know, trailers always show the best bit of the movie that's coming.

It never came. It was a movie that never opened. God didn't turn up. Still hasn't. Maybe that's why Mark suggested that as he hung on the cross, Jesus realised it wasn't going to come either, so he died in despair – without God:

'My God, my God, why hast thou forsaken me?' And Jesus uttered a loud cry and breathed his last.[14]

Earlier in this book I noticed how even twenty-five years after the curtains had closed on the death of Jesus, Paul and the other disciples were still waiting for them to open again and the second act to begin, the act in which God would complete the transcendental revolution begun by Jesus. To their disappointment and consternation, they too died waiting. The Christian Church is still waiting for the show to begin again. But the curtains remain firmly shut. Is that all that is left of the Jesus story then? Yet another apocalyptic failure? Another killing at Wounded Knee? And Jesus, another beguiling but defeated revolutionary? That is certainly an honest way to read the story. It is how many atheist admirers of Jesus read it. They always knew God would never arrive. How could he? He was never there in the first place. Are these our only choices then? Between a god who never turns up, and a god who was never there anyway?

Jesus left us with a consolatory hint of another way of reading his story. It is found in a book of his sayings that never made it into the official New Testament, called the Gospel of Thomas. This is what he said:

> His disciples said to him: 'When will the kingdom come?' Jesus said: 'It will not come by waiting for it. It will not be a matter of saying, "Here it is" or "There it is". Rather, the kingdom of the father is spread out upon the earth, and men do not see it.'[15]

The kingdom is already here but *we don't see it because we are looking in the wrong place*. We are looking to heaven, when we should be looking at earth. We are expecting God to do the work, when it is now up to us. Either because there is no God and never has been, or because God wants us to do the work *for the work's own sake*. Whichever way we read it, we are left with a distinction without a difference. It is the resistance that counts now, not who motivates it. Bonhoeffer got it right when he told us that we had to start acting *etsi deus non daretur* – as if God were not there. We have to change the world because it needs changing, not because of a divine command.

Jesus himself commended theism-of-the-deed and denounced theism-of-the-word.

> Not everyone who says to me, 'Lord, Lord,' shall enter the kingdom of heaven, but he who does the will of my Father who is in heaven.[16]

And what was it to do the will of the father? It was to welcome the stranger, feed the hungry, clothe the naked, and visit the sick and those in prison. If we did those things, *we did God*, even if *we did not believe in God.*

> . . . truly I say to you, as you did it to one of the least of these my brethren, you did it to me.[17]

To make the point doubly sure, he made it in its negative form as well. Those who believed in God but did not perform these merciful acts, whatever they thought they were doing, *they were not doing God*:

> . . . as you did it not to one of the least of these, you did it not to me.[18]

The force of these words from the Gospel of Matthew is strengthened by that saying of Jesus from the Gospel of Thomas – and their meaning is clear. Act II has started, but it is now up to us to take it forward. Either because there is no God to take the revolution on or because God always intended to do it through us. Whichever way you look at it, it amounts to the same thing. It is why atheists and theists can make common cause. It is the *work* that counts not the motivator. It still bears the two marks of the Jesus revolution. The interruptive power of forgiveness to reverse the world's chronic addiction to revenge. And a refusal to let the world's domination systems go on flattening those at the bottom of their pyramids of power. What Jesus called the 'kingdom' is already at work on the earth as a non-violent resistance movement, and we can join it anytime, anywhere. We join it not by reciting a creed, but by *doing something*. By reconciling with those we have hurt and forgiving those who have hurt us. By challenging cruelty in all its forms, religious as well as political. By committing random acts of subversive kindness. Above all, by challenging how the system goes on enriching the already-too-rich and impoverishing the already-too-poor. There are always some who are brave enough to dedicate their whole lives to the work of this downside-up, other kingdom. Then there are people like me who dip in and out of it as courage and occasion allow. That, too, is how it operates. It is only ever a gesture away. And a single gesture in a whole lifetime may, for some, be all that was ever possible. It won't be lost. It will find its mark. It never triumphs, this other kingdom, is never fully realised on earth. But nor is it ever utterly defeated.

The resistance goes on, though the Church that calls itself after Christ has rarely ever tried to join it, or never for long. Often it has done the opposite. It has followed the world's style in its own institutional life. It has been one of the cruellest and least forgiving institutions in history. Not only have its leaders dressed themselves in the garments of power, they have exercised power over the despised and rejected with the same icy indifference as any other domination system. There have been many examples of this paradox in Church history, but the greatest is that it was in the name of the crucified Jew it claimed to follow that the Church ignited a new and enduring persecution of his own people. The first move in this persecution was theological. Having expropriated the Hebrew scriptures for its own purposes, the Church went on to blame the Jews for not submitting to its belief that Judaism was merely the prologue to Christianity, a belief to which they must now yield and abandon their old traditions. This theological aggression soon led to active persecution, as bad theology often does, and a new chapter in the long suffering of the Jews was opened, a chapter that is still being written. As one of them put it:

> The Christians say they love Christ, but I think they hate him without knowing it; so they take the cross by the other end and make a sword out of it and strike us with it! You understand Golda . . . they take the cross and turn it around, they turn it around my God.[19]

No, the Church never really tried to live the Jesus-life. What it did was to keep his story alive. Even as they shifted uncomfortably in their seats, Christians were compelled to listen to it. Week after week and day after day, the story was read to them. And it has always provoked some of them to try to live it. To follow the way of radical, revolutionary forgiveness. To see the world as it appears from the bottom looking up, not from the top looking down. To try to live by the story of the magnificent defeat of

Jesus, the godforsaken revolutionary.

That's why I remain a member of the Christian Church. I want to be part of the community that keeps the dangerous memory of Jesus alive in history. But not out of nostalgia. Only because it can make a difference. Because practising forgiveness in human affairs, at both the personal and political level, is one of the few ways humans can effectively redirect the crushing momentum of their own violent history. Because forgiveness offers us the possibility of improvising a different script for ourselves, a different story. In theological jargon, of *saving* ourselves and the little blue planet that came into existence five billion years ago and slowly gave us life.

That, and because Jesus also invites us to active sympathy for those who become the casualties of the planet's propulsive and indifferent force – those who suffer. Not in order to find an answer to the *problem* of suffering, but to respond to those who do the suffering. Maybe there never ever was any love behind the universe. No creative intelligence that brought it into being in order to love it and be loved by it. Maybe it all just happened because it happened. An effect without a cause. Nevertheless, in time love also happened. Another effect without a cause? Who cares? Parse it any way you like. Reduce it to neurology. Mutual self-protection. Wherever it came from, it is the most beautiful and revolutionary force in human history. And it asks each of us a question. Jesus posed it long before Auden, but Auden's version will do: *why can't the more loving one be me?*

I am a Christian because this is the story I try to live by. I am not suggesting that this way of following Jesus should convince you or anyone else. I am no longer in the convincing business. It's just that this is the story I now try feebly to live by. And that makes me a Christian. It's just that I am a Christian without God. I follow Jesus *etsi deus non daretur.*

Sorry Ivan: I am holding on to the ticket.

ACKNOWLEDGEMENTS

I finished the final copy-editing stage of this book in the middle of March 2020 during the Coronavirus pandemic and the international panic that accompanied it. As a man in his eighties who was reckoned to be part of the population thought to be at the greatest risk of catching and dying from the virus, it was a strangely eschatological time to be finishing a book, and I wondered if I would live long enough to see it published. By the time you read this we'll know!

In many ways, the situation we are facing is one the book was trying to think about. The strange character of the human animal, with its capacity for hatred and destruction, in tension with its capacity for heroic love and kindness. That's why I was moved when our neighbour Martin across the street emailed us to ask if he could help us with shopping or any other kind of support, when or if we were forced into isolating ourselves. He got the message of the book without having read it, though maybe he'd already read W.H. Auden:

If equal affection cannot be,
Let the more loving one be me.

Any writer owes an enormous debt to his editors, and I have three to thank. My daughter Sara gave it an expert first reading and suggested changes to the text and to the tone, all of which I accepted. Then Simon Thorogood, my editor at Canongate, gave the book two detailed and careful readings. Again, I benefited enormously from his suggested changes, all of which made it a much better book, though its defects are all my own.

Then came the copy-edit, conducted by Octavia Reeve, whose edits and challenges improved the book even more.

I am grateful to them all.

I am also extremely grateful to my affectionate and intensely supportive agent Caroline Dawnay, and her colleague Sophie Scard.

I am grateful to Don Paterson for sending me that fragment of a great poem by Richard Wilbur:

Is there some huge attention, do you think,
Which suffers us and is inviolate,
To which all hearts are open, which remarks
The sparrow's weighty fall, and overhears
In the worst rancour a deflected sweetness?
I should be glad to know it.

ENDNOTES

All Bible quotations are from the Revised Standard Version unless otherwise noted.

Prologue

1. Didion, Joan. *The White Album*. London: 4th Estate, 2017, p. 13.
2. Wiesel, Elie. *Night*. New York: Hill and Wang, 1972, p. 64.
3. Molodowsky, Kadya. *Modern Poems on the Bible*. Philadelphia and Jerusalem: The Jewish Publication Society, 1994, p. 167.
4. Dostoevsky, Fyodor. *The Brothers Karamazov*, translated by Richard Pevear and Larissa Volokhonsky. New York: Everyman's Library, 1990, p. 244.
5. Boethius. In: *Medieval Latin Lyrics*, translated by Helen Waddell. London: Constable, 1933, p. 49.
6. Dostoevsky, *The Brothers Karamazov*, p. 245.
7. Auden, W.H. 'September 1, 1939'. In: *Another Time*. London: Random House, 1940.
8. Nietzsche, Friedrich. 'What Is the Meaning of Ascetic Ideals?', *Genealogy of Morals*, Third Essay, Section 15.

In: *Basic Writings of Nietzsche*, translated by Walter Kaufmann. New York: The Modern Library, 1992, p. 563.

9. Freud, Sigmund. *Civilization and its Discontents*. London: Penguin Books, 1991, p. 305.

10. Hume, David. *Essays and Treatises on Several Subjects, Volume 2: The Natural History of Religion, Section III*. Edinburgh: Blackwood, 1825, p. 392.

Chapter 1

1. Kuhn, Thomas. *The Structure of Scientific Revolutions*. Chicago: University of Chicago Press, 1970, p. 10.

2. Levi, Primo. *In the Beginning, Modern Poems on the Bible*. Philadelphia and Jerusalem: The Jewish Publication Society, 1994, p. 29.

3. Bryson, Bill. *A Short History of Nearly Everything*. London and New York: Doubleday, 2003, p. 115.

4. Levi. *In the Beginning: Modern Poems on the Bible*, p. 29.

5. Dickinson, Emily. 'This World Is Not Conclusion' (Poem 501). In: *The Complete Poems of Emily Dickinson*. Boston and Toronto: Little, Brown and Company, 1960, p. 243.

6. Phillips, Adam. *On Balance*. London: Hamish Hamilton, 2010, p. 46.

Chapter 2

1. Pembrey, Marcus. 'A User's Guide'. In: *The Troubled Helix*, edited by T. Marteau and M. Richards. Cambridge: Cambridge University Press, 1996.

2. Bloom, Harold. *Possessed by Memory: The Inward Light of Criticism*. New York: Alfred A. Knopf, 2019, p. 107.

3. Puchner, Martin. *The Written World: How Literature Shaped History*. London: Granta, 2017, p. ix.

4. Scott, Laura. *So Many Rooms*. Manchester: Carcanet, 2019, p. 2.

5. Holloway, Richard. *A Little History of Religion*. New Haven and London: Yale University Press, 2016, pp. 4ff.

6. MacNeice, Louis. 'Snow'. In: *Collected Poems*. London: Faber and Faber, 1979, p. 30.

7. Polkinghorne, John. *Reason and Reality: The Relationship between Science and Religion*. London: SPCK, 1991, pp. 40ff.

8. Thomas, R.S. 'Via Negativa'. In: *Collected Poems*. London: Dent, 1993, p. 220.

9. Crews, Frederick. 'Saving Us from Darwin', Part 1. *The New York Times Review of Books*, 4 October 2001.

10. Hick, John. *The Fifth Dimension*. Oxford: One Word, 1999, p. 42.

11. Macaulay, Thomas Babington. *The History of England*, Vol. I. Leipzig: Bernard Tauchnitz, 1849, p. 96.

12. Crawford, Robert. 'Advice'. In: *Full Volume*. London: Cape Poetry, 2008, p. 1.

Chapter 3

1. Jenkins, Peter. Quoted in the *Independent*.

2. Scruton, Roger. *The Face of God*. London: Bloomsbury, 2012, p. 17.

3. Gray, John. *Seven Types of Atheism*. London: Penguin, 2019, p. 26.

4. Scruton, Roger. *The Uses of Pessimism*. Oxford: Oxford University Press, 2010, p. 17.

5. Rée, Jonathan. *Witcraft: The Invention of Philosophy in English*. London: Allen Lane, 2019, p. 39.
6. Didion, *The White Album*, p. 206.
7. Joel, 3:14.
8. Yeats, W.B. 'The Second Coming'. In: *The Poems*. London: Everyman, 1998, p. 235.
9. Manchester, William. *The Last Lion: Winston Spencer Churchill, Visions of Glory 1874–1932*. Boston: Little Brown and Company, 1983, p. 650.

Chapter 4

1. Rée, *Witcraft*, pp. 7–9.
2. Genesis, 1:1–31; 2:1–3.
3. Barton, John, *A History of the Bible: The Book and its Faiths*. London: Allen Lane, 2019, p. 476.
4. II Timothy, 3:16.

Chapter 5

1. Genesis, 2:4–25; 3:1–24.
2. II Samuel, 12:1–7.
3. Nietzsche, Friedrich. *The Birth of Tragedy*. London: Penguin Classics, 1993, p. 53.
4. I Corinthians, 15:21–22.
5. Romans, 5:12–17.
6. I Corinthians, 15:51–52.
7. I Timothy, 2:11–15.
8. Brown, Peter. *Augustine of Hippo*. London: Faber and Faber, 1967, p. 388.
9. Brown, Peter. *The Body and Society*. London: Faber and Faber, 1990, p. 424.
10. Sirach, 25:24–26.

11. Osborne, Lawrence. *The Poisoned Embrace*. London: Vintage 1994, p. 68.

12. Blake, William. 'I Went to the Garden of Love' (Poem 16). In: *Songs of Experience*. London, 1794.

Chapter 6

1. Prideaux, Sue. *I am Dynamite: A Life of Friedrich Nietzsche*. London: Faber and Faber, 2019, p. 87.

2. Didion, Joan. *Slouching Towards Bethlehem*. New York: Farrar, Straus and Giroux, 1968, p. 127.

3. Didion, *Slouching*, p. 120.

4. Carter, John. In *Atlantic Monthly*, 1920. Quoted in: Lucy Moore, *Anything Goes: A Biography of the Roaring Twenties*. London: Atlantic Books, 2008, p. 234.

5. Moore, *Anything Goes*, p. 235.

6. Leckey, Mark. Quoted in *Tate Etc.*, Autumn 2019, p. 76.

7. Leckey, *Tate Etc.*, p. 82.

8. Roszak, Theodore. *The Making of a Counter Culture*. London: Faber and Faber, 1971, p. 240.

9. Roszak, *The Making of a Counter Culture*, p. 251.

10. Genesis, 1:28.

11. Roszak, *The Making of a Counter Culture*, p. 226.

12. Roszak, *The Making of a Counter Culture*, p. 231.

13. Genesis, 2:16–17.

14. Pollan, Michael. *How to Change Your Mind: The New Science of Psychedelics*. London: Allen Lane, 2018, p. 2.

15. Pollan, *How to Change Your Mind*, pp. 2–3.

16. Pollan, *How to Change Your Mind*, p. 58.

17. Ehrenreich, Barbara. *Natural Causes: Life, Death and the Illusion of Control*. London: Granta, 2018, p. 202.

18. James, William. *Varieties of Religious Experience: A Study*

in Human Nature. London: Longmans, Green and Co., 1828, p. 380.

19. James, *Varieties of Religious Experience*, p. 386.
20. James, *Varieties of Religious Experience*, p. 388.
21. Pollan, *How to Change Your Mind*, p. 17.
22. Pollan, *How to Change Your Mind*, p. 25.
23. Pollan, *How to Change Your Mind*, p. 85.
24. Pollan, *How to Change Your Mind*, p. 136.

Chapter 7

1. Svetāsvatara Upanishad, 2:8ff. In: *Sacred Texts of the World: A Universal Anthology*, edited by Ninian Smart and Richard D. Hecht. London: Quercus, 2007, p. 213.
2. Maitrī Upanishad, 6:18ff. In: *Sacred Texts of the World*, p. 214.
3. James, *Varieties of Religious Experience*, p. 401.
4. Weil, Simone. *An Anthology*. New York: Grove Press, 1986, pp. 240.
5. James, *Varieties of Religious Experience*, p. 408.
6. James, *Varieties of Religious Experience*, p. 411.
7. James, *Varieties of Religious Experience*, p. 416.
8. James, *Varieties of Religious Experience*, p. 417.
9. James, *Varieties of Religious Experience*, p. 419.
10. Astley, Jeff. 'Background to Research into Religious and Spiritual Experience'. Warwick: Warwick University, 2017–20. <https://warwick.ac.uk/fac/soc/ces/research/wreru/aboutus/staff/ja/jeff_astley_background_to_research_into_spiritual_and_religious_experience.pdf>
11. Greeley, Andrew. Survey undertaken at the Centre for the Study of American Pluralism, National Opinion Research Centre, University of Chicago, 1975.

12. Muir, Edwin. 'Transfiguration'. In: *The Collected Poems of Edwin Muir*. London: Faber and Faber, 1960, p. 198.

13. James, *Varieties of Religious Experience*, p. 388.

14. Rée, *Witcraft*, pp. 7–9.

15. Baggini, Julian. *How the World Thinks: A Global History of Philosophy*. London: Granta, 2018, p. 79.

16. Baggini, *How the World Thinks*, p. 79.

17. Baggini, *How the World Thinks*, p. 82.

18. Rorty, Richard. *Philosophy and Social Hope*. London: Penguin, 1992, p. 84.

19. Dickinson, Hugh. In a letter to the author.

Chapter 8

1. Dostoevsky, *The Brothers Karamazov*, p. 244.

2. Johnston, Mark. *Saving God: Religion After Idolatry*, Princeton and Oxford: Princeton University Press, 2009, p. 181.

3. Strawson, Galen. 'Religion is a Sin', *London Review of Books*, 2 June 2011.

4. Job, 1:13–22.

5. Job, 19:25–26. *Revised English Bible*.

6. Scott, Ruth. *Between Living and Dying*. Edinburgh: Birlinn, 2019, p. 159.

7. Calvin, John. *Institutes of the Christian Religion*, Volume 1, Book II, Chapter I. Edinburgh, 1845, p. 289.

8. Romans, 8:28–30.

9. Calvin, John. *Institutes of the Christian Religion*, Volume 2, Book III, Chapter XXI. Edinburgh, 1845, p. 534.

10. Hogg, James. *The Private Memoirs and Confessions of a Justified Sinner*. Edinburgh: Canongate Classics, 1990, p. 100.

11. 'Predestination': Sura 9, Sura 36 and Hadith. In *Sacred Texts of the World*, pp. 163–4.

Chapter 9

1. Nietzsche, *Genealogy of Morals*. Second Essay, Section 6. p. 501.

2. Foucault, Michel. *Discipline and Punish: The Birth of the Prison*, translated from the French by Alan Sheridan. New York: Vintage Books, 1995, p. 1ff.

3. Proverbs, 3:11–12. *King James Bible*.

4. Hebrews, 12:4–7.

5. Gray, Alasdair. *Revelations: Personal Responses to the Books of the Bible*. Edinburgh: Canongate, 2005, p. 181.

6. There is a good discussion of all the theories mentioned here in *The Oxford Companion to Christian Thought*. Oxford: Oxford University Press, 2000, p. 687.

7. Genesis, 1:28.

8. Hick, John. *Evil and the God of Love*. New York: Harper and Row, 1966, p. 317.

9. Wilbur, Richard. 'The Mind Reader'. In: *The Mind Reader*. New York: Harcourt Brace Jovanovich, 1976. Poem begins p. 57, passage cited p. 63.

10. Waugh, Evelyn. *Brideshead Revisited*. London: Penguin Books, 1951, p. 288.

11. Bonhoeffer, Dietrich. *Letters and Papers from Prison*. London: SCM, 1971, p. 369.

12. Bonhoeffer, *Letters and Papers from Prison*, p. 279.

13. Mark, 10:45.

14. I Peter, 5:7.

15. Waddell, Helen. *Peter Abelard*. London: Constable, 1933, p. 199.

16. Psalms, 103:13.

17. Auden, W.H. 'The More Loving One'. In: *Collected Poems*. London: Faber and Faber, 1976, p. 445.

Chapter 10

1. Barton, John; *A History of the Bible,* London: Allan Lane, 2019, p. 311.

2. Mark, 1:9.

3. Mark, 6:2–3.

4. Crossan, John Dominic. *Jesus: A Revolutionary Biography.* San Francisco: Harper, 1995, p. 25.

5. Daniel, 7:13–14.

6. Matthew, 6:9–12.

7. Exodus, 21:23–25.

8. Matthew, 5:38–45.

9. Matthew, 5:3–10.

10. Crossan, *Jesus,* p. 62.

11. Matthew, 23:27.

12. Crossan, *Jesus,* p. 127.

13. Crossan, *Jesus,* p. 125.

14. Mark, 15:34 and 37.

15. Thomas, 113, in *The Complete Gospels*, Editor Robert J. Miller, New York, 1994, p. 322.

16. Matthew, 7:21.

17. Matthew, 25:40.

18. Matthew, 25:45.

19. Schwarz-Bart, André. *The Last of the Just.* London: Penguin, 1977, p. 332.

PERMISSION CREDITS

INDEX

INDEX